50 Diabetic-Friendly Dessert Recipes for Home

By: Kelly Johnson

Table of Contents

- Sugar-Free Cheesecake
- Almond Flour Brownies
- Avocado Chocolate Mousse
- Coconut Flour Cookies
- Chia Seed Pudding
- Greek Yogurt Parfait
- Low-Carb Lemon Bars
- Pumpkin Spice Mug Cake
- Berry Sorbet
- Almond Butter Cups
- Zucchini Bread
- Raspberry Almond Thumbprint Cookies
- Matcha Green Tea Ice Cream
- Cocoa-Dusted Almonds
- Cinnamon Apple Crisp
- Sugar-Free Popsicles
- Cauliflower Rice Pudding
- Dark Chocolate Bark with Nuts
- Coconut Milk Custard
- Peanut Butter Banana Bites
- Lemon Ricotta Pancakes
- Vanilla Bean Panna Cotta
- Ginger Turmeric Cookies
- Pistachio Rosewater Macarons
- Spiced Carrot Cake
- Blueberry Chia Seed Jam
- Chocolate Avocado Pudding
- Almond Joy Energy Bites
- Mocha Hazelnut Mousse
- Mango Coconut Rice Pudding
- Blackberry Lime Sorbet
- Pumpkin Pie Bites
- Caramelized Banana Slices
- Hazelnut Flourless Cake
- Orange Cardamom Cookies
- Berry Compote with Yogurt

- Pistachio Crusted Yogurt Bars
- Chocolate Covered Strawberries
- Maple Pecan Blondies
- Tiramisu Cups
- Key Lime Pie Jars
- Cacao Nib Rice Crispy Treats
- Peach Ginger Sorbet
- Almond Flour Shortbread
- Vegan Chocolate Truffles
- Strawberry Basil Gelato
- Apple Cinnamon Rice Pudding
- Blueberry Cheesecake Bites
- Chocolate Mint Avocado Cookies
- Coconut Flour Donuts

Sugar-Free Cheesecake

Ingredients:

For the crust:

- 1 1/2 cups almond flour
- 1/4 cup melted butter
- 1-2 tablespoons powdered erythritol (or any other sugar substitute of your choice)
- 1/2 teaspoon vanilla extract
- Pinch of salt

For the filling:

- 24 oz (680g) cream cheese, softened
- 1 cup sour cream
- 3/4 cup powdered erythritol (adjust to taste)
- 3 large eggs
- 1 tablespoon lemon juice
- 1 teaspoon vanilla extract
- Optional: Fresh berries or sugar-free berry sauce for topping

Instructions:

1. Preheat your oven to 325°F (160°C).
2. Make the crust:
    - In a mixing bowl, combine almond flour, melted butter, powdered erythritol, vanilla extract, and a pinch of salt. Mix until well combined and crumbly.
    - Press the mixture firmly into the bottom of a greased 9-inch (23 cm) springform pan, forming an even layer.
3. Bake the crust in the preheated oven for 10-12 minutes, until lightly golden. Remove from oven and let it cool while you prepare the filling.
4. Make the filling:
    - In a large mixing bowl, beat the softened cream cheese until smooth.
    - Add sour cream, powdered erythritol, eggs, lemon juice, and vanilla extract. Beat until well combined and creamy. Taste and adjust sweetness if needed by adding more powdered erythritol.
5. Assemble and bake:
    - Pour the filling over the cooled crust in the springform pan. Smooth the top with a spatula.
6. Bake the cheesecake in the oven at 325°F (160°C) for about 45-55 minutes, or until the edges are set and the center is slightly jiggly.
7. Cooling and chilling:
    - Turn off the oven and crack the oven door open. Let the cheesecake cool in the oven for about an hour.

- Remove the cheesecake from the oven and run a knife around the edges of the pan to loosen it from the sides.
 - Chill the cheesecake in the refrigerator for at least 4 hours, preferably overnight, to firm up.
8. Serve:
 - Once chilled and firm, remove the cheesecake from the springform pan.
 - Serve slices plain or with fresh berries or sugar-free berry sauce on top.

Enjoy your sugar-free cheesecake! Adjust sweetness to your preference and feel free to experiment with different sugar substitutes or crust variations if desired.

Almond Flour Brownies

Ingredients:

- 1 cup almond flour
- 1/2 cup cocoa powder
- 1/2 teaspoon baking powder
- 1/4 teaspoon salt
- 1/2 cup unsalted butter, melted (or coconut oil for dairy-free)
- 3/4 cup granulated sugar (or coconut sugar for a less refined option)
- 2 large eggs, at room temperature
- 1 teaspoon vanilla extract
- 1/2 cup chocolate chips (optional, but recommended)

Instructions:

1. Preheat your oven to 350°F (175°C). Grease or line with parchment paper an 8x8 inch baking pan.
2. Mix dry ingredients: In a medium bowl, whisk together almond flour, cocoa powder, baking powder, and salt until well combined.
3. Combine wet ingredients: In a separate large bowl, mix melted butter (or coconut oil) with sugar until smooth. Add eggs one at a time, mixing well after each addition. Stir in vanilla extract.
4. Combine dry and wet ingredients: Gradually add the dry ingredients to the wet ingredients, stirring until just combined. Be careful not to overmix. Fold in chocolate chips if using.
5. Bake: Pour the batter into the prepared baking pan and spread it evenly with a spatula. Bake in the preheated oven for 20-25 minutes, or until a toothpick inserted into the center comes out with a few moist crumbs.
6. Cool and serve: Allow the brownies to cool completely in the pan on a wire rack before cutting into squares. Enjoy your almond flour brownies!

These brownies are rich, chocolatey, and have a slightly different texture than traditional brownies due to the almond flour. They're perfect for those who are gluten-sensitive or looking to incorporate more nut-based flours into their diet.

Avocado Chocolate Mousse

Ingredients:

- 2 ripe avocados
- 1/2 cup cocoa powder (unsweetened)
- 1/2 cup maple syrup or honey (adjust to taste)
- 1 teaspoon vanilla extract
- 1/4 cup milk (dairy or non-dairy, as per preference)
- A pinch of salt
- Optional toppings: whipped cream, berries, chopped nuts

Instructions:

1. Prepare avocados: Cut the avocados in half, remove the pits, and scoop out the flesh into a food processor or blender.
2. Blend: Add cocoa powder, maple syrup (or honey), vanilla extract, milk, and a pinch of salt to the avocado in the blender or food processor.
3. Blend until smooth: Process or blend until the mixture is creamy and smooth. Stop occasionally to scrape down the sides with a spatula to ensure everything is well combined.
4. Taste and adjust: Taste the mousse and adjust sweetness if needed by adding more maple syrup or honey.
5. Chill (optional): If you prefer a chilled mousse, refrigerate it for about 30 minutes to 1 hour before serving.
6. Serve: Spoon the avocado chocolate mousse into serving bowls or glasses. Optionally, top with whipped cream, berries, or chopped nuts for extra texture and flavor.
7. Enjoy: Serve immediately and enjoy this delicious and healthier alternative to traditional chocolate mousse!

This avocado chocolate mousse is rich in flavor, smooth in texture, and offers a unique twist with the avocado adding creaminess and healthy fats. It's a great dessert option for those looking for dairy-free or healthier dessert alternatives.

Coconut Flour Cookies

Ingredients:

- 1/2 cup coconut flour
- 1/2 cup coconut oil or unsalted butter, melted
- 1/2 cup honey or maple syrup (adjust to taste)
- 2 eggs, at room temperature
- 1 teaspoon vanilla extract
- 1/4 teaspoon salt
- Optional add-ins: chocolate chips, chopped nuts, dried fruit, etc.

Instructions:

1. Preheat your oven to 350°F (175°C). Line a baking sheet with parchment paper.
2. Mix wet ingredients: In a large bowl, whisk together melted coconut oil (or butter), honey (or maple syrup), eggs, and vanilla extract until well combined.
3. Combine dry ingredients: In a separate bowl, sift the coconut flour and salt together to break up any clumps.
4. Combine wet and dry ingredients: Gradually add the dry ingredients to the wet ingredients, stirring until a dough forms. The dough may be slightly sticky.
5. Fold in add-ins: If you're using chocolate chips, nuts, or any other add-ins, gently fold them into the dough until evenly distributed.
6. Form cookies: Using a spoon or cookie scoop, drop rounded tablespoons of dough onto the prepared baking sheet, spacing them about 2 inches apart. Use your hands to gently flatten each cookie slightly, as coconut flour cookies don't spread much during baking.
7. Bake: Bake in the preheated oven for 10-12 minutes, or until the edges are golden brown.
8. Cool and store: Allow the cookies to cool on the baking sheet for 5 minutes before transferring them to a wire rack to cool completely. Store in an airtight container at room temperature for up to 5 days.

Tips:

- Coconut flour tends to absorb more liquid than other flours, so it's important to measure accurately.
- If the dough seems too dry, you can add a tablespoon of milk or water at a time until the desired consistency is reached.
- Experiment with different add-ins like shredded coconut, dried cranberries, or cinnamon for added flavor variations.

These coconut flour cookies are soft, slightly chewy, and have a lovely coconut flavor. They're a great option for those following a gluten-free or grain-free diet, and they make a tasty treat for any occasion!

Chia Seed Pudding

Ingredients:

- 1/4 cup chia seeds
- 1 cup milk of your choice (almond milk, coconut milk, soy milk, etc.)
- 1-2 tablespoons sweetener (maple syrup, honey, agave syrup, etc.), optional
- 1/2 teaspoon vanilla extract, optional

Instructions:

1. Mix: In a bowl or jar, combine the chia seeds, milk, sweetener (if using), and vanilla extract (if using). Stir well to combine.
2. Rest: Let the mixture sit for 5 minutes to allow the chia seeds to begin absorbing the liquid. Stir again to break up any clumps of chia seeds.
3. Chill: Cover the bowl or jar and refrigerate for at least 2 hours, or preferably overnight. This allows the chia seeds to absorb the liquid and develop a pudding-like consistency.
4. Serve: Stir the chia seed pudding before serving to redistribute the seeds. Serve chilled, topped with fruits, nuts, granola, or any other toppings you like.

Variations:

- Chocolate Chia Seed Pudding: Add 1-2 tablespoons of cocoa powder or chocolate syrup to the basic recipe before chilling.
- Fruit Flavored Chia Seed Pudding: Blend fresh or frozen fruits (such as berries, mango, or banana) with the milk before mixing with chia seeds.
- Matcha Chia Seed Pudding: Whisk 1 teaspoon of matcha powder into the milk before mixing with chia seeds.
- Peanut Butter Chia Seed Pudding: Stir 1-2 tablespoons of peanut butter into the basic recipe before chilling.
- Spiced Chia Seed Pudding: Add a pinch of ground cinnamon, nutmeg, or cardamom to the basic recipe for a warm, spiced flavor.

Tips:

- The ratio of chia seeds to liquid in the basic recipe can be adjusted to achieve your desired thickness. More chia seeds will yield a thicker pudding.
- Sweeteners and flavors can be adjusted to suit your taste preferences. Taste the mixture before chilling and adjust as needed.
- Chia seed pudding can be stored in the refrigerator for up to 3-4 days. Stir before serving leftovers, as the pudding may thicken further over time.

Chia seed pudding is not only delicious but also packed with fiber, protein, and healthy fats, making it a satisfying and nutritious choice for any time of day!

Greek Yogurt Parfait

Ingredients:

- 1 cup Greek yogurt (plain or flavored, your choice)
- 1/2 cup granola (homemade or store-bought)
- 1 cup mixed fresh fruits (berries, banana slices, mango chunks, etc.)
- Honey or maple syrup (optional, for drizzling)
- Nuts or seeds (optional, for topping)

Instructions:

1. Prepare your ingredients: Have your Greek yogurt, granola, and fruits washed, chopped, and ready to use.
2. Layering the parfait:
    - Start with a layer of Greek yogurt at the bottom of a serving glass or bowl.
    - Add a layer of granola on top of the yogurt. You can use any type of granola you prefer, whether it's plain, honey-nut, or with added fruits and nuts.
    - Add a layer of mixed fresh fruits over the granola. Choose a variety of colorful fruits for both visual appeal and different flavors.
    - Repeat the layers until you reach near the top of the glass or bowl, finishing with a final layer of Greek yogurt.
3. Top it off:
    - Drizzle honey or maple syrup over the top layer of yogurt for added sweetness, if desired.
    - Sprinkle nuts or seeds on top for extra crunch and texture. Sliced almonds, chopped walnuts, or pumpkin seeds work well.
4. Serve:
    - Serve immediately and enjoy your delicious Greek yogurt parfait!

Tips for Customization:

- Flavor Variations: You can use flavored Greek yogurt like vanilla, honey, or fruit-flavored varieties for added taste.
- Toppings: Experiment with different toppings such as shredded coconut, dried fruits, or a sprinkle of cinnamon.
- Nutritional Boost: Add a tablespoon of chia seeds or ground flax seeds between the layers for extra fiber and omega-3 fatty acids.
- Make it Vegan: Substitute Greek yogurt with dairy-free yogurt alternatives such as almond milk yogurt or coconut milk yogurt.

Greek yogurt parfaits are not only satisfying but also packed with protein, probiotics (if using yogurt with live cultures), fiber, and vitamins from the fruits and nuts. They make a perfect breakfast, snack, or even a light dessert option!

Low-Carb Lemon Bars

Crust Ingredients:

- 1 cup almond flour
- 1/4 cup coconut flour
- 1/4 cup powdered erythritol (or sweetener of your choice)
- 1/4 teaspoon salt
- 1/4 cup unsalted butter, melted

Lemon Filling Ingredients:

- 4 large eggs
- 3/4 cup powdered erythritol (or sweetener of your choice)
- 1/2 cup fresh lemon juice (about 3-4 lemons)
- 1 tablespoon lemon zest
- 1/4 cup almond flour
- 1/2 teaspoon baking powder
- Powdered erythritol (or sweetener), for dusting (optional)

Instructions:

1. Preheat your oven to 350°F (175°C). Line an 8x8 inch baking pan with parchment paper, leaving some overhang for easy removal later.
2. Make the crust:
    - In a mixing bowl, combine almond flour, coconut flour, powdered erythritol, and salt.
    - Stir in melted butter until the mixture resembles coarse crumbs.
    - Press the crust mixture evenly into the bottom of the prepared baking pan.
3. Bake the crust:
    - Bake in the preheated oven for 12-15 minutes, or until lightly golden brown. Remove from oven and let it cool slightly while you prepare the filling.
4. Make the lemon filling:
    - In a large bowl, whisk together eggs and powdered erythritol until well combined.
    - Add lemon juice, lemon zest, almond flour, and baking powder. Whisk until smooth and well incorporated.
5. Pour over the crust:
    - Pour the lemon filling over the baked crust, spreading it out evenly.
6. Bake the lemon bars:
    - Bake for 20-25 minutes, or until the filling is set and the edges are lightly golden brown.
7. Cool and chill:
    - Remove from the oven and let the lemon bars cool completely in the pan on a wire rack. Once cooled, refrigerate for at least 2 hours (or overnight) to firm up.

8. Serve:
    - Lift the chilled lemon bars out of the pan using the parchment paper overhang. Dust with powdered erythritol (if desired) and cut into squares before serving.
9. Store:
    - Store any leftovers in an airtight container in the refrigerator for up to 5 days.

Tips:

- Sweetener: Adjust the amount of sweetener according to your taste preferences. Taste the filling mixture before baking and add more sweetener if needed.
- Zest: Use a fine grater to zest the lemons for the best flavor. Avoid grating the bitter white pith beneath the yellow skin.
- Variations: You can add a touch of vanilla extract to the filling for additional flavor depth.

These low-carb lemon bars are refreshing, tangy, and make a wonderful dessert or snack option for those following a low-carb or keto diet. Enjoy the bright citrus flavors without the guilt of excessive carbs!

Pumpkin Spice Mug Cake

Ingredients:

- 4 tablespoons almond flour
- 1 tablespoon coconut flour
- 1 tablespoon granulated sweetener of your choice (such as erythritol, stevia, or monk fruit)
- 1/4 teaspoon baking powder
- 1/2 teaspoon pumpkin pie spice (or a mix of cinnamon, nutmeg, ginger, and cloves)
- Pinch of salt
- 2 tablespoons pumpkin puree (canned or homemade)
- 1 large egg
- 1 tablespoon coconut oil or melted butter
- 1/2 teaspoon vanilla extract

Instructions:

1. Prepare the mug: Grease a microwave-safe mug with coconut oil or butter.
2. Mix dry ingredients: In the mug, whisk together almond flour, coconut flour, sweetener, baking powder, pumpkin pie spice, and salt until well combined.
3. Add wet ingredients: Add pumpkin puree, egg, melted coconut oil or butter, and vanilla extract to the mug. Mix well until smooth and no lumps remain.
4. Microwave: Microwave on high for 1.5 to 2 minutes, or until the cake is set and springs back slightly when touched. Cooking time may vary depending on your microwave's wattage.
5. Cool and enjoy: Allow the mug cake to cool for a minute or two before digging in. Optionally, top with whipped cream, a sprinkle of cinnamon, or a drizzle of sugar-free maple syrup.

Tips:

- Make sure to use a large enough mug to allow for rising during cooking.
- Adjust sweetness according to your taste preferences by adding more or less sweetener.
- For a dairy-free option, use coconut oil instead of butter.
- You can customize this mug cake by adding chopped nuts or chocolate chips to the batter before microwaving.

This pumpkin spice mug cake is moist, flavorful, and perfect for a cozy dessert or snack, especially during the fall season when pumpkin spice flavors are popular. Enjoy it warm straight from the mug!

Berry Sorbet

Ingredients:

- 3 cups mixed berries (such as strawberries, blueberries, raspberries)
- 1/2 cup granulated sugar (adjust according to sweetness of berries and preference)
- 1/4 cup water
- 1 tablespoon freshly squeezed lemon juice
- Optional: fresh berries, mint leaves, or lemon zest for garnish

Instructions:

1. Prepare the berries: If using fresh berries, wash them thoroughly. If using frozen berries, allow them to thaw slightly.
2. Make the simple syrup: In a small saucepan, combine the granulated sugar and water over medium heat. Stir until the sugar is completely dissolved, creating a simple syrup. Remove from heat and let it cool to room temperature.
3. Blend the berries: In a blender or food processor, combine the mixed berries, cooled simple syrup, and freshly squeezed lemon juice. Blend until smooth and well combined.
4. Strain (optional): For a smoother sorbet, strain the mixture through a fine-mesh sieve to remove any seeds or pulp. Press down gently with a spatula to extract all the liquid.
5. Chill the mixture: Transfer the berry mixture to a bowl or container and refrigerate for at least 1 hour, or until thoroughly chilled.
6. Churn in ice cream maker (optional): If you have an ice cream maker, churn the chilled berry mixture according to the manufacturer's instructions until it reaches a sorbet consistency, usually about 20-30 minutes.
7. Freeze without ice cream maker: If you don't have an ice cream maker, pour the chilled berry mixture into a shallow dish. Place it in the freezer and stir every 30 minutes with a fork to break up ice crystals until it reaches a sorbet-like consistency, about 2-3 hours.
8. Serve: Scoop the berry sorbet into serving bowls or glasses. Garnish with fresh berries, mint leaves, or a sprinkle of lemon zest if desired. Serve immediately and enjoy!

Tips:

- Experiment with different combinations of berries for varying flavors and colors.
- Adjust the sweetness level by adding more or less sugar depending on the sweetness of your berries.
- For a quicker sorbet, use already chilled berries and serve straight from the blender without additional freezing.

This berry sorbet is light, fruity, and naturally sweetened, making it a healthier alternative to traditional ice cream. It's perfect for enjoying the vibrant flavors of summer or any time you crave a refreshing treat!

Almond Butter Cups

Ingredients:

- For the chocolate coating:
    - 1 cup dark chocolate chips or chopped dark chocolate (preferably 70% cocoa or higher)
    - 1 tablespoon coconut oil
- For the almond butter filling:
    - 1/2 cup almond butter (smooth or crunchy, as per preference)
    - 2 tablespoons powdered sugar or sweetener of your choice
    - 1/2 teaspoon vanilla extract
    - Pinch of salt

Instructions:

1. Prepare the almond butter filling:
    - In a small bowl, mix together almond butter, powdered sugar (or sweetener), vanilla extract, and a pinch of salt until smooth and well combined. Taste and adjust sweetness if needed.
2. Melt the chocolate:
    - In a microwave-safe bowl or using a double boiler, melt the dark chocolate chips or chopped dark chocolate with coconut oil until smooth and fully melted. Stir well to combine.
3. Line muffin tin or use molds:
    - Line a muffin tin with paper liners or use silicone molds for easy removal.
4. Assemble the almond butter cups:
    - Spoon a small amount of melted chocolate into each muffin cup, just enough to cover the bottom. Use the back of a spoon to spread the chocolate slightly up the sides of the cup.
5. Add the almond butter filling:
    - Place a small dollop (about 1 teaspoon) of almond butter filling in the center of each chocolate-coated cup.
6. Cover with more chocolate:
    - Pour or spoon the remaining melted chocolate over the almond butter filling, covering it completely and smoothing out the top with the back of a spoon.
7. Chill to set:
    - Place the muffin tin or molds in the refrigerator for about 30 minutes, or until the almond butter cups are firm and set.
8. Serve and enjoy:
    - Once set, remove the almond butter cups from the muffin tin or molds. Peel off any paper liners if using. Serve and enjoy these delicious almond butter cups!

Tips:

- Storage: Store almond butter cups in an airtight container in the refrigerator for up to 2 weeks. They can also be stored in the freezer for longer shelf life.
- Variations: Experiment with different nut butters like cashew or hazelnut butter. You can also sprinkle sea salt on top of the chocolate before it sets for a sweet and salty flavor combination.
- Customization: Use milk chocolate or white chocolate if you prefer a sweeter taste, adjusting the sweetness level accordingly.

These homemade almond butter cups are decadent, rich, and perfect for satisfying your chocolate cravings with a nutty twist. Enjoy making and indulging in these delightful treats!

Zucchini Bread

Ingredients:

- 1 1/2 cups grated zucchini (about 1 medium zucchini)
- 1 cup all-purpose flour
- 1/2 cup whole wheat flour (or use all-purpose flour if preferred)
- 1 teaspoon baking powder
- 1/2 teaspoon baking soda
- 1/2 teaspoon salt
- 1 teaspoon ground cinnamon
- 1/4 teaspoon ground nutmeg (optional)
- 1/2 cup unsalted butter, melted (or substitute with vegetable oil)
- 1/2 cup granulated sugar
- 1/2 cup brown sugar (packed)
- 2 large eggs, at room temperature
- 1 teaspoon vanilla extract
- Optional: 1/2 cup chopped nuts (walnuts or pecans), chocolate chips, or raisins

Instructions:

1. Preheat your oven to 350°F (175°C). Grease a 9x5 inch loaf pan or line it with parchment paper for easy removal.
2. Grate the zucchini: Use a box grater to grate the zucchini. Wrap the grated zucchini in a clean kitchen towel and squeeze out excess moisture. Measure out 1 1/2 cups of grated zucchini.
3. Mix dry ingredients: In a medium bowl, whisk together the all-purpose flour, whole wheat flour (or additional all-purpose flour), baking powder, baking soda, salt, cinnamon, and nutmeg (if using). Set aside.
4. Mix wet ingredients: In a large bowl, whisk together the melted butter, granulated sugar, and brown sugar until well combined. Add the eggs, one at a time, whisking well after each addition. Stir in the vanilla extract.
5. Combine: Gradually add the dry ingredients to the wet ingredients, stirring with a wooden spoon or spatula until just combined. Fold in the grated zucchini and optional add-ins (nuts, chocolate chips, or raisins), if using. Do not overmix.
6. Bake: Pour the batter into the prepared loaf pan and smooth the top with a spatula. Bake in the preheated oven for 50-60 minutes, or until a toothpick inserted into the center comes out clean or with a few moist crumbs.
7. Cool: Allow the zucchini bread to cool in the pan for 10 minutes, then remove it from the pan and transfer it to a wire rack to cool completely.
8. Slice and serve: Once cooled, slice the zucchini bread and serve. Enjoy it warm or at room temperature.

Tips:

- Add-ins: Customize your zucchini bread by adding chopped nuts (like walnuts or pecans), chocolate chips, or raisins for extra texture and flavor.
- Storage: Store leftover zucchini bread in an airtight container at room temperature for up to 3 days, or refrigerate for longer freshness.
- Freezing: Zucchini bread freezes well. Wrap slices or the whole loaf tightly in plastic wrap and aluminum foil before freezing. Thaw at room temperature when ready to enjoy.

This zucchini bread recipe is a great way to use up surplus zucchini from your garden or local market, resulting in a moist and flavorful loaf that's perfect for breakfast or a snack any time of day!

Raspberry Almond Thumbprint Cookies

Ingredients:

- 1 cup unsalted butter, softened
- 2/3 cup granulated sugar
- 1 teaspoon vanilla extract
- 1/2 teaspoon almond extract
- 2 cups all-purpose flour
- 1/2 teaspoon salt
- 3/4 cup finely ground almonds (almond flour or almond meal)
- Raspberry jam (or any jam of your choice)

Instructions:

1. Preheat your oven to 350°F (175°C). Line baking sheets with parchment paper or silicone baking mats.
2. Cream butter and sugar: In a large bowl, cream together the softened butter and granulated sugar until light and fluffy using a hand mixer or stand mixer with a paddle attachment.
3. Add extracts: Mix in the vanilla extract and almond extract until well combined.
4. Combine dry ingredients: In a separate bowl, whisk together the all-purpose flour, salt, and finely ground almonds (almond flour or almond meal).
5. Mix dough: Gradually add the dry ingredients to the butter mixture, mixing on low speed until a dough forms. Scrape down the sides of the bowl as needed to ensure even mixing.
6. Form cookies: Roll the dough into 1-inch balls and place them on the prepared baking sheets, spacing them about 2 inches apart.
7. Make thumbprints: Use your thumb or the back of a teaspoon to make an indentation in the center of each cookie. Make sure not to press all the way through.
8. Fill with jam: Spoon a small amount of raspberry jam (or your preferred flavor) into each indentation, filling it almost to the top.
9. Bake: Bake the cookies in the preheated oven for 12-14 minutes, or until the edges are lightly golden.
10. Cool: Allow the cookies to cool on the baking sheets for a few minutes, then transfer them to a wire rack to cool completely.
11. Serve and enjoy: Once cooled, these raspberry almond thumbprint cookies are ready to be enjoyed. Store any leftovers in an airtight container at room temperature.

Tips:

- Jam selection: Feel free to use any flavor of jam or preserves you prefer, such as strawberry, apricot, or even lemon curd for a different twist.

- Texture: The finely ground almonds add a nice texture to these cookies. If you prefer a smoother texture, you can use almond flour instead of grinding your own almonds.
- Variations: For a festive touch, you can dust the cookies with powdered sugar once they have cooled completely.

These raspberry almond thumbprint cookies are perfect for holiday gatherings, afternoon tea, or any time you crave a sweet and nutty treat. Enjoy the combination of almond and raspberry flavors in each bite!

Matcha Green Tea Ice Cream

Ingredients:

- 2 cups heavy cream
- 1 cup whole milk
- 3/4 cup granulated sugar
- 2 tablespoons matcha green tea powder
- 4 large egg yolks
- 1 teaspoon vanilla extract
- Optional: 1/4 teaspoon almond extract (for added flavor complexity)

Instructions:

1. Prepare the ice cream base:
    - In a medium saucepan, combine the heavy cream, whole milk, and granulated sugar over medium heat. Whisk until the sugar is dissolved and the mixture is just starting to simmer (do not boil).
2. Whisk in matcha powder:
    - Remove the saucepan from heat. Whisk in the matcha green tea powder until it is fully incorporated and there are no lumps.
3. Temper the egg yolks:
    - In a separate bowl, whisk the egg yolks until smooth. Gradually add about 1 cup of the warm matcha cream mixture into the egg yolks, whisking constantly. This process is called tempering and prevents the eggs from scrambling.
4. Combine and cook:
    - Pour the tempered egg yolk mixture back into the saucepan with the remaining matcha cream mixture. Return the saucepan to medium heat.
5. Cook until thickened:
    - Cook the mixture over medium heat, stirring constantly with a wooden spoon or heatproof spatula, until the mixture thickens slightly and coats the back of the spoon (about 5-7 minutes). Do not let it boil.
6. Strain the mixture (optional):
    - For a smoother texture, strain the custard through a fine-mesh sieve into a clean bowl to remove any cooked egg bits or undissolved matcha powder.
7. Cool the custard:
    - Stir in the vanilla extract (and almond extract, if using). Let the custard cool to room temperature, then cover with plastic wrap directly on the surface of the custard to prevent a skin from forming. Chill in the refrigerator for at least 4 hours or overnight until thoroughly chilled.
8. Churn the ice cream:
    - Once chilled, pour the matcha custard into your ice cream maker and churn according to the manufacturer's instructions until it reaches a soft-serve consistency.

9. **Freeze:**
   - Transfer the churned ice cream into an airtight container. Press a piece of wax paper or parchment paper onto the surface of the ice cream to prevent ice crystals from forming. Freeze for at least 4 hours or until firm.
10. **Serve and enjoy:**
    - Scoop the matcha green tea ice cream into bowls or cones. Garnish with additional matcha powder or whipped cream if desired. Enjoy this creamy and flavorful homemade treat!

Tips:

- Matcha quality: Use high-quality matcha powder for the best flavor and color.
- Texture: For a smoother texture, ensure the custard is cooked gently and strained before chilling.
- Variations: Experiment with toppings such as crushed toasted almonds or a drizzle of honey for added texture and sweetness.

Homemade matcha green tea ice cream is a delicious way to enjoy the unique flavor of matcha while cooling off on a hot day or after a meal. It's a treat that's sure to impress with its vibrant color and rich taste!

Cocoa-Dusted Almonds

Ingredients:

- 1 cup whole almonds
- 1 tablespoon cocoa powder (unsweetened)
- 2 tablespoons powdered sugar (optional, adjust sweetness to taste)
- 1/4 teaspoon vanilla extract
- Pinch of salt

Instructions:

1. Toast the almonds (optional):
   - Preheat your oven to 350°F (175°C). Spread the almonds in a single layer on a baking sheet. Toast in the oven for about 8-10 minutes, stirring halfway through, until they are lightly golden and fragrant. Remove from the oven and let them cool completely.
2. Prepare the coating:
   - In a medium bowl, combine the cocoa powder, powdered sugar (if using), vanilla extract, and a pinch of salt. Mix well until thoroughly combined.
3. Coat the almonds:
   - Add the cooled almonds to the bowl with the cocoa mixture. Toss and stir gently until the almonds are evenly coated with the cocoa mixture. You can use a spoon or your hands to coat them thoroughly.
4. Set and cool:
   - Spread the cocoa-dusted almonds in a single layer on a parchment-lined baking sheet or a clean surface. Let them sit for about 10-15 minutes to allow the cocoa coating to set.
5. Store or serve:
   - Once the cocoa coating has set, transfer the cocoa-dusted almonds to an airtight container or enjoy them immediately as a delicious snack.

Tips:

- Adjust sweetness: If you prefer sweeter almonds, increase the amount of powdered sugar. Taste the coating mixture and adjust according to your preference.
- Variations: You can customize the flavor by adding a pinch of cinnamon or a dash of cayenne pepper for a spicy kick.
- Storage: Store cocoa-dusted almonds in an airtight container at room temperature for up to 2 weeks. They can also be stored in the refrigerator for longer shelf life.

These cocoa-dusted almonds are perfect for satisfying your sweet cravings while providing a nutritious snack option. Enjoy them on their own, or add them to yogurt, salads, or trail mix for an extra crunch and cocoa flavor!

Cinnamon Apple Crisp

Ingredients:

For the Apple Filling:

- 6 cups peeled and sliced apples (about 6 medium apples, such as Granny Smith or Honeycrisp)
- 1/4 cup granulated sugar
- 1 tablespoon all-purpose flour
- 1 teaspoon ground cinnamon
- 1/4 teaspoon ground nutmeg (optional)
- 1 tablespoon lemon juice

For the Crisp Topping:

- 1 cup old-fashioned rolled oats
- 1/2 cup all-purpose flour
- 1/2 cup packed light brown sugar
- 1/2 teaspoon ground cinnamon
- 1/4 teaspoon salt
- 1/2 cup unsalted butter, cold and cut into small pieces

Instructions:

1. Preheat your oven to 350°F (175°C). Grease a 9x9 inch baking dish or a similar sized dish with butter or non-stick cooking spray.
2. Prepare the apple filling:
    - In a large bowl, combine the sliced apples, granulated sugar, flour, cinnamon, nutmeg (if using), and lemon juice. Toss until the apples are evenly coated.
3. Make the crisp topping:
    - In another bowl, combine the rolled oats, flour, brown sugar, cinnamon, and salt. Mix well.
    - Add the cold butter pieces to the oat mixture. Using a pastry cutter, fork, or your fingers, cut the butter into the dry ingredients until the mixture resembles coarse crumbs and the butter is evenly distributed.
4. Assemble the crisp:
    - Spread the apple mixture evenly in the prepared baking dish.
    - Sprinkle the crisp topping over the apples, covering them completely and pressing down gently.
5. Bake:
    - Place the baking dish in the preheated oven and bake for 40-45 minutes, or until the topping is golden brown and the apples are tender and bubbling.
6. Cool and serve:

- Remove the cinnamon apple crisp from the oven and let it cool for at least 10-15 minutes before serving. Serve warm with vanilla ice cream or whipped cream, if desired.

Tips:

- Apple selection: Choose apples that are firm and slightly tart for the best texture and flavor in the crisp. Mixing different types of apples can also add complexity to the dish.
- Topping variations: Feel free to add chopped nuts (such as pecans or walnuts) or a dash of ground ginger or cloves to the crisp topping for extra flavor.
- Storage: Leftover apple crisp can be covered and stored in the refrigerator for up to 3 days. Reheat in the oven or microwave before serving.

This cinnamon apple crisp is a wonderful dessert for any occasion, especially during the fall when apples are in season. Enjoy the combination of warm, spiced apples and crunchy oat topping for a comforting treat!

Sugar-Free Popsicles

Ingredients:

- 2 cups fresh or frozen fruit (such as berries, mango, pineapple, or a combination)
- 1-2 tablespoons lemon juice (optional, for a hint of tartness)
- 1-2 tablespoons honey or maple syrup (optional, adjust sweetness to taste)
- 1 cup plain Greek yogurt or coconut milk (for creaminess, optional)

Instructions:

1. Prepare the fruit:
   - Wash and chop the fresh fruit if using. If using frozen fruit, thaw slightly.
2. Blend the ingredients:
   - In a blender or food processor, combine the fruit, lemon juice (if using), and honey or maple syrup (if using). Blend until smooth. Taste and adjust sweetness as desired.
3. Add creaminess (optional):
   - For a creamy texture, add plain Greek yogurt or coconut milk to the fruit mixture. Blend again until smooth and well combined.
4. Fill popsicle molds:
   - Pour the fruit mixture into popsicle molds, leaving a little space at the top for expansion. Insert popsicle sticks into each mold.
5. Freeze:
   - Place the popsicle molds in the freezer and freeze until solid, about 4-6 hours or overnight.
6. Unmold and serve:
   - To unmold the popsicles, run the molds under warm water for a few seconds to loosen them. Gently pull out the popsicles and serve immediately.

Tips for Sugar-Free Popsicles:

- Sweeteners: Instead of honey or maple syrup, you can use sugar substitutes like erythritol, stevia, or monk fruit sweetener. Adjust the amount according to your taste preferences.
- Variations: Experiment with different fruits and flavor combinations. Add chunks of fresh fruit, herbs (like mint or basil), or even a splash of fruit juice for added flavor.
- Creamy options: Use Greek yogurt for a protein boost and creamy texture, or coconut milk for a dairy-free and vegan option.
- Texture: For a chunkier texture, blend the fruit mixture less or add chopped fruit pieces directly into the molds before freezing.
- Storage: Store leftover popsicles in an airtight container or resealable plastic bags in the freezer. They should keep well for up to 1 month.

These sugar-free popsicles are not only delicious but also a healthier alternative to store-bought versions, making them perfect for cooling off on hot days or as a guilt-free dessert option. Enjoy making and customizing these refreshing treats!

Cauliflower Rice Pudding

Ingredients:

- 1 medium head of cauliflower (about 4 cups of cauliflower rice)
- 2 cups unsweetened almond milk (or any milk of your choice)
- 1/4 cup heavy cream (or coconut cream for dairy-free)
- 1/4 cup granulated sweetener (such as erythritol, stevia, or monk fruit)
- 1 teaspoon vanilla extract
- 1/2 teaspoon ground cinnamon
- Pinch of salt
- Optional toppings: chopped nuts, fresh berries, cinnamon powder

Instructions:

1. Prepare the cauliflower rice:
    - Cut the cauliflower into florets and pulse in a food processor until it resembles rice grains. You should have about 4 cups of cauliflower rice.
2. Cook the cauliflower rice:
    - In a medium saucepan, combine the cauliflower rice with almond milk (or your preferred milk) over medium heat. Bring to a simmer and cook for about 5-7 minutes, stirring occasionally, until the cauliflower is tender and cooked through.
3. Add sweetener and flavors:
    - Stir in the heavy cream (or coconut cream), granulated sweetener, vanilla extract, ground cinnamon, and a pinch of salt. Continue to cook over medium heat for another 5-7 minutes, stirring frequently, until the mixture thickens to a pudding-like consistency.
4. Adjust sweetness:
    - Taste and adjust sweetness as needed by adding more sweetener if desired.
5. Serve:
    - Remove from heat and let the cauliflower rice pudding cool slightly. Serve warm or chilled.
6. Optional toppings:
    - Garnish with chopped nuts, fresh berries, or a sprinkle of cinnamon powder before serving, if desired.

Tips:

- Texture: The cauliflower rice should be cooked until tender but not mushy. Adjust cooking time accordingly.
- Sweeteners: Choose a sweetener that suits your dietary preferences. Adjust the amount based on how sweet you like your pudding.
- Variations: Add other flavors like nutmeg, cardamom, or almond extract for different flavor profiles.

- Storage: Store leftover cauliflower rice pudding in an airtight container in the refrigerator for up to 3 days. Reheat gently before serving if desired.

This cauliflower rice pudding is a creative and healthy alternative to traditional rice pudding, perfect for those looking to reduce carbohydrates or incorporate more vegetables into their diet. Enjoy this creamy and satisfying dessert!

Dark Chocolate Bark with Nuts

Ingredients:

- 12 ounces dark chocolate (70% cocoa or higher), chopped into small pieces
- 1 cup mixed nuts (such as almonds, walnuts, pecans), roughly chopped
- Optional: 1/4 teaspoon sea salt (for sprinkling on top)

Instructions:

1. Prepare a baking sheet:
    - Line a baking sheet with parchment paper or a silicone baking mat. Set aside.
2. Melt the dark chocolate:
    - Place the chopped dark chocolate in a heatproof bowl. You can melt the chocolate using one of these methods:
        - Microwave: Heat in 30-second intervals, stirring well after each interval, until the chocolate is melted and smooth.
        - Double boiler: Place the bowl over a pot of simmering water (make sure the bowl doesn't touch the water). Stir the chocolate occasionally until melted.
3. Spread the chocolate:
    - Once melted and smooth, pour the dark chocolate onto the prepared baking sheet. Use a spatula to spread it into an even layer, about 1/4 inch thick.
4. Add the nuts:
    - Sprinkle the chopped nuts evenly over the melted chocolate. Gently press the nuts into the chocolate so they adhere well.
5. Optional: Sprinkle with sea salt:
    - If desired, sprinkle a little sea salt over the top of the chocolate bark for a sweet and salty flavor contrast.
6. Set the bark:
    - Allow the chocolate bark to cool at room temperature until completely set and hardened. You can speed up the process by placing it in the refrigerator for about 30 minutes.
7. Break into pieces:
    - Once the chocolate is completely set, use a sharp knife or your hands to break the bark into pieces of your desired size and shape.
8. Serve and store:
    - Serve the dark chocolate bark with nuts as a delicious treat or package it in an airtight container. Store in a cool, dry place for up to 2 weeks.

Tips:

- Chocolate selection: Use high-quality dark chocolate with at least 70% cocoa for the best flavor and texture.

- Nuts: Customize the bark with your favorite nuts or a combination. Toast the nuts beforehand for extra flavor.
- Variations: Experiment with adding dried fruits, coconut flakes, or a drizzle of melted white chocolate for decoration.

Dark chocolate bark with nuts makes a wonderful homemade gift or a delightful treat for any occasion. Enjoy the combination of rich chocolate and crunchy nuts in every bite!

Coconut Milk Custard

Ingredients:

- 1 can (14 ounces) full-fat coconut milk
- 1/2 cup granulated sugar
- 4 large egg yolks
- 1/4 cup cornstarch
- 1/4 teaspoon salt
- 1 teaspoon vanilla extract
- Optional: Shredded coconut, toasted coconut flakes, or fresh berries for garnish

Instructions:

1. Prepare the custard base:
    - In a medium saucepan, whisk together the coconut milk and granulated sugar over medium heat until the sugar dissolves and the mixture is smooth and heated through.
2. Whisk the egg yolks:
    - In a separate bowl, whisk together the egg yolks, cornstarch, and salt until smooth and well combined.
3. Temper the eggs:
    - Gradually pour about half of the warm coconut milk mixture into the egg yolk mixture, whisking constantly to temper the eggs. This prevents them from curdling.
4. Combine and cook:
    - Pour the tempered egg mixture back into the saucepan with the remaining coconut milk mixture. Cook over medium heat, whisking constantly, until the mixture thickens and comes to a gentle boil. This should take about 5-7 minutes.
5. Add vanilla extract:
    - Remove the saucepan from the heat and stir in the vanilla extract. Mix well.
6. Strain (optional):
    - If desired, strain the custard through a fine-mesh sieve to remove any lumps or cooked egg bits. This step will give you a smoother texture.
7. Chill:
    - Transfer the coconut milk custard to a heatproof bowl and let it cool slightly. Cover the surface of the custard with plastic wrap to prevent a skin from forming. Chill in the refrigerator for at least 2 hours, or until completely chilled and set.
8. Serve:
    - Spoon the chilled coconut milk custard into individual serving bowls or glasses. Garnish with shredded coconut, toasted coconut flakes, or fresh berries if desired.
9. Enjoy:
    - Serve and enjoy the creamy and coconutty goodness of this dairy-free custard!

Tips:

- Coconut milk: Use full-fat coconut milk for a richer and creamier custard.
- Sweetness: Adjust the amount of sugar according to your taste preference.
- Variations: Experiment with adding coconut flakes or coconut essence for more coconut flavor.
- Storage: Store leftover coconut milk custard in an airtight container in the refrigerator for up to 3 days.

This coconut milk custard is a delightful dessert that's perfect for those who enjoy coconut flavors and are looking for a dairy-free or vegan option. It's creamy, comforting, and sure to satisfy your sweet tooth!

Peanut Butter Banana Bites

Ingredients:

- 2 large bananas, peeled and cut into thick slices
- 1/4 cup peanut butter (creamy or crunchy, depending on your preference)
- Optional toppings: chopped nuts, shredded coconut, chocolate chips, chia seeds

Instructions:

1. Prepare the bananas:
    - Peel the bananas and cut them into thick slices, about 1/2 inch thick.
2. Spread peanut butter:
    - Take each banana slice and spread a thin layer of peanut butter on one side. You can use creamy or crunchy peanut butter based on your preference for texture.
3. Optional toppings:
    - Sprinkle your choice of optional toppings over the peanut butter. This could include chopped nuts (like almonds or walnuts), shredded coconut, chocolate chips, or chia seeds for added crunch and flavor.
4. Assemble:
    - Place another banana slice on top of the peanut butter-covered slice to create a sandwich.
5. Serve or freeze:
    - Serve the peanut butter banana bites immediately for a soft and creamy treat, or place them in the freezer for about 30 minutes to 1 hour to firm up if you prefer a colder snack.
6. Enjoy:
    - Enjoy these peanut butter banana bites as a nutritious snack or dessert. They are perfect for satisfying cravings for something sweet and satisfying!

Tips:

- Banana selection: Choose ripe but firm bananas for easier slicing and handling.
- Variations: Experiment with different nut butters like almond butter or cashew butter for variety.
- Storage: If you have leftovers, store them in an airtight container in the refrigerator for up to 2 days. If frozen, they can be kept for longer and enjoyed as a chilled treat.

These peanut butter banana bites are not only delicious but also packed with potassium, healthy fats, and protein, making them a great option for a quick energy boost or a post-workout snack. Enjoy the combination of creamy peanut butter and sweet bananas in every bite!

Lemon Ricotta Pancakes

Ingredients:

- 1 cup all-purpose flour
- 1 tablespoon granulated sugar
- 1 teaspoon baking powder
- 1/2 teaspoon baking soda
- 1/4 teaspoon salt
- 1 cup ricotta cheese
- 3/4 cup milk
- 2 large eggs
- Zest of 1 lemon
- 2 tablespoons fresh lemon juice
- 1 teaspoon vanilla extract
- Butter or oil for cooking

Instructions:

1. Prepare dry ingredients:
   - In a large bowl, whisk together the flour, sugar, baking powder, baking soda, and salt.
2. Prepare wet ingredients:
   - In another bowl, whisk together the ricotta cheese, milk, eggs, lemon zest, lemon juice, and vanilla extract until well combined and smooth.
3. Combine wet and dry ingredients:
   - Pour the wet ingredients into the bowl with the dry ingredients. Gently fold the mixture together with a spatula until just combined. Be careful not to overmix; a few lumps are okay.
4. Heat the griddle or skillet:
   - Heat a griddle or large non-stick skillet over medium heat. Add a small amount of butter or oil and spread it evenly.
5. Cook the pancakes:
   - Pour about 1/4 cup of batter onto the heated griddle for each pancake. Use the back of a spoon or measuring cup to spread the batter into a circle if needed. Cook until bubbles form on the surface of the pancake and the edges begin to look set, about 2-3 minutes.
6. Flip and cook:
   - Carefully flip the pancakes and cook on the other side until golden brown and cooked through, about 1-2 minutes more.
7. Serve:
   - Transfer the cooked pancakes to a plate and keep warm. Repeat with the remaining batter, adding more butter or oil to the griddle as needed.
8. Enjoy:

- Serve the lemon ricotta pancakes warm with maple syrup, fresh berries, a dusting of powdered sugar, or additional lemon zest on top.

Tips:

- **Ricotta cheese:** Use whole milk ricotta for a creamier texture in the pancakes.
- **Lemon flavor:** Adjust the amount of lemon zest and juice according to your preference for a stronger or milder lemon flavor.
- **Fluffy pancakes:** Folding the batter gently and not overmixing will help keep the pancakes light and fluffy.

These lemon ricotta pancakes are perfect for a special weekend breakfast or brunch. They are rich, tangy, and have a wonderful texture that makes them a favorite among pancake lovers. Enjoy making and savoring these delightful pancakes!

Vanilla Bean Panna Cotta

Ingredients:

- 1 cup whole milk
- 2 cups heavy cream
- 1/2 cup granulated sugar
- 1 vanilla bean pod (or 2 teaspoons pure vanilla extract)
- 2 1/4 teaspoons powdered gelatin (or 1 packet, about 7 grams)
- 3 tablespoons cold water

Optional Garnishes:

- Fresh berries
- Mint leaves
- Caramel sauce
- Chocolate shavings

Instructions:

1. Prepare the gelatin:
   - In a small bowl, sprinkle the gelatin over the cold water. Let it sit for about 5-10 minutes to bloom and soften.
2. Prepare the vanilla bean:
   - Split the vanilla bean pod lengthwise with a sharp knife. Scrape out the seeds using the back of the knife.
3. Make the panna cotta mixture:
   - In a medium saucepan, combine the whole milk, heavy cream, granulated sugar, and the scraped vanilla bean seeds (or vanilla extract if using). Heat over medium heat, stirring occasionally, until the mixture is hot but not boiling, and the sugar has dissolved. Remove from heat.
4. Incorporate the gelatin:
   - Add the softened gelatin mixture to the hot cream mixture. Stir until the gelatin is completely dissolved.
5. Strain the mixture (optional):
   - For a smoother texture, strain the mixture through a fine-mesh sieve into a pouring jug or directly into serving glasses to remove any bits of vanilla bean or undissolved gelatin.
6. Pour into molds or glasses:
   - Divide the panna cotta mixture evenly among serving glasses or molds. If using molds, lightly grease them with flavorless oil (like vegetable or coconut oil) to ease unmolding later.
7. Chill and set:

- Refrigerate the panna cotta for at least 4 hours, or until fully set. For best results, allow it to chill overnight.
8. Serve:
    - To serve, gently run a knife around the edge of each mold or glass. Carefully invert the panna cotta onto serving plates if using molds. Alternatively, serve the panna cotta directly in glasses.
9. Garnish:
    - Garnish the vanilla bean panna cotta with fresh berries, mint leaves, a drizzle of caramel sauce, or chocolate shavings if desired.

Tips:

- Vanilla bean: If using vanilla extract instead of a vanilla bean pod, add it after removing the cream mixture from heat to preserve its flavor.
- Setting time: Ensure the panna cotta has enough time to set properly in the refrigerator before serving.
- Storage: Store leftover panna cotta in the refrigerator, covered, for up to 3 days.

This vanilla bean panna cotta is smooth, creamy, and luxurious, making it a perfect dessert for special occasions or as an elegant finish to any meal. Enjoy the delicate vanilla flavor and silky texture of this classic Italian treat!

Ginger Turmeric Cookies

Ingredients:

- 1/2 cup unsalted butter, softened
- 1/2 cup brown sugar, packed
- 1/4 cup granulated sugar
- 1 large egg
- 1 teaspoon vanilla extract
- 1 cup all-purpose flour
- 1/2 teaspoon baking soda
- 1/2 teaspoon ground ginger
- 1/2 teaspoon ground turmeric
- 1/4 teaspoon ground cinnamon
- 1/4 teaspoon salt
- Optional: 1/4 cup crystallized ginger, finely chopped (for extra ginger flavor and texture)

Instructions:

1. Preheat oven and prepare baking sheet:
   - Preheat your oven to 350°F (175°C). Line a baking sheet with parchment paper or silicone baking mat.
2. Cream butter and sugars:
   - In a large bowl, cream together the softened butter, brown sugar, and granulated sugar until light and fluffy.
3. Add egg and vanilla:
   - Beat in the egg and vanilla extract until well combined.
4. Combine dry ingredients:
   - In a separate bowl, whisk together the flour, baking soda, ground ginger, ground turmeric, ground cinnamon, and salt.
5. Mix wet and dry ingredients:
   - Gradually add the dry ingredients to the wet ingredients, mixing until just combined. If using crystallized ginger, fold it into the cookie dough at this stage.
6. Form cookie dough:
   - Scoop rounded tablespoons of dough and roll them into balls. Place them on the prepared baking sheet, spacing them about 2 inches apart.
7. Flatten cookies:
   - Use the bottom of a glass or the palm of your hand to gently flatten each cookie ball.
8. Bake:
   - Bake in the preheated oven for 10-12 minutes, or until the edges are lightly golden. The centers may still look slightly soft, but they will continue to set as they cool.
9. Cool and enjoy:

- Allow the cookies to cool on the baking sheet for a few minutes before transferring them to a wire rack to cool completely.
10. Store:
    - Once cooled, store the ginger turmeric cookies in an airtight container at room temperature for up to 1 week.

Tips:

- Adjust spices: Feel free to adjust the amount of ground ginger and turmeric according to your taste preferences.
- Crystallized ginger: If using crystallized ginger, ensure it's finely chopped to evenly distribute throughout the cookies.
- Flavor variations: You can add a pinch of black pepper for a hint of spice or a tablespoon of orange zest for citrus notes.

These ginger turmeric cookies are not only delicious but also offer a warming and aromatic experience with each bite. They're perfect for enjoying with a cup of tea or coffee, and they bring a unique twist to your cookie repertoire!

Pistachio Rosewater Macarons

Ingredients:

For the Macaron Shells:

- 100 grams aged egg whites (about 3 large eggs)
- 50 grams granulated sugar
- 200 grams powdered sugar
- 110 grams almond flour
- 30 grams finely ground pistachios (blanched, unsalted)
- Green food coloring (optional)

For the Pistachio Filling:

- 1/2 cup unsalted butter, softened
- 1 cup powdered sugar
- 1/4 cup finely ground pistachios (blanched, unsalted)
- 1-2 teaspoons rosewater (adjust to taste)
- Green food coloring (optional)

Instructions:

Making the Macaron Shells:

1. Prepare baking sheets: Line two baking sheets with parchment paper or silicone mats. Have a piping bag fitted with a round tip (about 1/2 inch in diameter) ready.
2. Prepare dry ingredients: In a bowl, sift together the powdered sugar, almond flour, and finely ground pistachios. Discard any larger almond pieces that stay in the sieve.
3. Whip the egg whites: In a clean, dry mixing bowl, whip the aged egg whites on medium speed until foamy. Gradually add the granulated sugar while continuing to whip. Increase speed to high and whip until stiff peaks form. Optionally, add a few drops of green food coloring during this stage for a light green color.
4. Macaronage: Gently fold the dry ingredients into the whipped egg whites using a spatula. Use about 50 strokes to combine, folding until the batter is smooth and flows slowly off the spatula in ribbons. Be careful not to overmix.
5. Pipe and rest: Transfer the batter to the prepared piping bag. Pipe 1.5-inch circles onto the prepared baking sheets, spacing them about 1 inch apart. Tap the baking sheets firmly on the counter to release any air bubbles. Let the piped macarons rest at room temperature for 30-60 minutes, until a skin forms on the surface and they are no longer sticky to the touch.
6. Bake: Preheat the oven to 300°F (150°C). Bake the macarons, one sheet at a time, for 15-18 minutes, rotating halfway through baking. The macarons should have developed feet, be set but not browned, and easily lift off the parchment paper. Let them cool completely on the baking sheets before carefully peeling them off.

Making the Pistachio Rosewater Filling:

1. Cream butter: In a mixing bowl, beat the softened butter until creamy and smooth.
2. Add powdered sugar and pistachios: Gradually add the powdered sugar and finely ground pistachios, beating until well combined and fluffy.
3. Flavor with rosewater: Add rosewater, 1 teaspoon at a time, tasting after each addition until desired flavor is achieved. Add a drop of green food coloring if desired for a light green hue.
4. Assembly: Pair similar-sized macaron shells together. Pipe or spoon a small amount of the pistachio rosewater filling onto the flat side of one shell and gently sandwich with another shell. Repeat with remaining macaron shells.
5. Maturation: Place filled macarons in an airtight container and refrigerate for 24-48 hours. This allows the flavors to meld and the texture to soften, resulting in a better eating experience.
6. Serve and enjoy: Bring macarons to room temperature before serving for the best texture and flavor. They can be stored in the refrigerator for up to 5 days.

Tips:

- Aging egg whites: Age egg whites at room temperature for 24-48 hours, or use freshly separated egg whites and let them sit at room temperature for 30 minutes to 1 hour before whipping.
- Pistachios: Ensure pistachios are finely ground to prevent lumps in the macaron shells and filling.
- Rosewater: Adjust the amount of rosewater according to your preference for a subtle or pronounced floral flavor.
- Consistency: Consistency in macaron batter is key; it should be thick enough to pipe but not runny.

These pistachio rosewater macarons are perfect for special occasions or as a unique treat to impress guests. They combine the nuttiness of pistachios with the delicate floral notes of rosewater, creating a sophisticated and delicious dessert experience. Enjoy making and savoring these delightful French treats!

Spiced Carrot Cake

Ingredients:

For the Cake:

- 2 cups all-purpose flour
- 1 teaspoon baking powder
- 1 teaspoon baking soda
- 1/2 teaspoon salt
- 1 teaspoon ground cinnamon
- 1/2 teaspoon ground ginger
- 1/4 teaspoon ground nutmeg
- 1/4 teaspoon ground cloves
- 1 cup granulated sugar
- 1 cup brown sugar, packed
- 1 cup vegetable oil or melted coconut oil
- 4 large eggs
- 2 teaspoons vanilla extract
- 3 cups grated carrots (about 4-5 medium carrots)
- 1 cup chopped walnuts or pecans (optional)

For the Cream Cheese Frosting:

- 8 ounces cream cheese, softened
- 1/2 cup unsalted butter, softened
- 4 cups powdered sugar
- 1 teaspoon vanilla extract

Optional Garnish:

- Chopped nuts (walnuts or pecans)
- Shredded coconut
- Carrot curls

Instructions:

For the Cake:

1. Preheat oven and prepare pans: Preheat your oven to 350°F (175°C). Grease and flour two 9-inch round cake pans, or line them with parchment paper.
2. Prepare dry ingredients: In a medium bowl, whisk together the flour, baking powder, baking soda, salt, cinnamon, ginger, nutmeg, and cloves until well combined.

3. Mix wet ingredients: In a large bowl, whisk together the granulated sugar, brown sugar, and oil until combined. Add the eggs one at a time, whisking well after each addition. Stir in the vanilla extract.
4. Combine dry and wet ingredients: Gradually add the dry ingredients to the wet ingredients, mixing until just combined. Fold in the grated carrots and chopped nuts (if using) until evenly distributed throughout the batter.
5. Bake: Divide the batter evenly between the prepared cake pans. Smooth the tops with a spatula. Bake in the preheated oven for 25-30 minutes, or until a toothpick inserted into the center comes out clean.
6. Cool: Allow the cakes to cool in the pans for 10 minutes before transferring them to a wire rack to cool completely.

For the Cream Cheese Frosting:

1. Mix cream cheese and butter: In a large bowl, beat the softened cream cheese and butter together until smooth and creamy.
2. Add powdered sugar and vanilla: Gradually add the powdered sugar, one cup at a time, beating well after each addition. Stir in the vanilla extract until smooth and creamy.
3. Frost the cake: Once the cakes are completely cool, place one cake layer on a serving plate or cake stand. Spread a layer of cream cheese frosting over the top. Place the second cake layer on top and frost the top and sides of the cake with the remaining frosting.
4. Optional garnish: Garnish with chopped nuts, shredded coconut, or carrot curls if desired.
5. Serve and store: Slice and serve the spiced carrot cake at room temperature. Store any leftover cake covered in the refrigerator for up to 5 days.

Tips:

- Carrots: Use freshly grated carrots for the best texture and flavor.
- Nuts: Feel free to omit nuts if you prefer a nut-free cake or substitute with raisins or shredded coconut.
- Spices: Adjust the amount of spices according to your preference for a more or less spiced cake.
- Frosting: For a lighter frosting, you can reduce the amount of powdered sugar or use whipped cream cheese.

This spiced carrot cake with cream cheese frosting is a perfect dessert for celebrations or gatherings, offering a balance of warm spices, sweetness from carrots, and richness from the cream cheese frosting. Enjoy baking and indulging in this delicious homemade treat!

Blueberry Chia Seed Jam

Ingredients:

- 2 cups fresh or frozen blueberries
- 2-3 tablespoons maple syrup or honey (adjust to taste)
- 2 tablespoons chia seeds
- 1 tablespoon fresh lemon juice
- 1/2 teaspoon vanilla extract (optional)

Instructions:

1. Cook the blueberries: In a medium saucepan, heat the blueberries over medium heat. If using fresh blueberries, add a tablespoon of water to help create steam. Cook until the blueberries begin to break down and release their juices, about 5-7 minutes.
2. Mash the blueberries: Mash the blueberries with a fork or potato masher to your desired consistency. If you prefer a smoother jam, you can blend the mixture with an immersion blender or transfer it to a regular blender.
3. Add sweetener and flavorings: Stir in the maple syrup or honey, adjusting the amount to your desired sweetness. Add the chia seeds, lemon juice, and vanilla extract (if using), stirring well to combine.
4. Simmer and thicken: Continue to cook the mixture over medium-low heat for another 5-10 minutes, stirring frequently. The chia seeds will absorb the liquid and help thicken the jam. Remove from heat when the jam reaches your desired consistency. Keep in mind that it will continue to thicken as it cools.
5. Cool and store: Let the blueberry chia seed jam cool completely before transferring it to a jar or airtight container. Store in the refrigerator for up to 2 weeks.

Tips:

- Frozen blueberries: If using frozen blueberries, there's no need to add water at the beginning as they will release their own juices once heated.
- Sweetness: Adjust the amount of maple syrup or honey according to your taste and the sweetness of your blueberries.
- Texture: For a smoother jam, blend the mixture after cooking. For a chunkier jam, simply mash the blueberries lightly.

Blueberry chia seed jam is delicious on toast, pancakes, yogurt, or as a filling for pastries. It's packed with antioxidants from the blueberries and omega-3 fatty acids from the chia seeds, making it a healthy addition to your breakfast or snack options. Enjoy the vibrant flavor and texture of this homemade jam!

Chocolate Avocado Pudding

Ingredients:

- 2 ripe avocados
- 1/2 cup cocoa powder (unsweetened)
- 1/2 cup maple syrup or honey (adjust to taste)
- 1/3 cup milk (dairy or non-dairy, such as almond milk)
- 1 teaspoon vanilla extract
- Pinch of salt
- Optional toppings: Fresh berries, sliced bananas, chopped nuts, shredded coconut

Instructions:

1. Prepare the avocados: Cut the avocados in half, remove the pits, and scoop out the flesh into a food processor or blender.
2. Add ingredients: Add the cocoa powder, maple syrup or honey, milk, vanilla extract, and a pinch of salt to the food processor or blender.
3. Blend until smooth: Blend the ingredients until completely smooth and creamy, scraping down the sides of the blender or food processor as needed to ensure everything is well combined.
4. Adjust sweetness: Taste the pudding and adjust the sweetness by adding more maple syrup or honey if desired.
5. Chill: Transfer the pudding to a bowl or individual serving dishes and chill in the refrigerator for at least 30 minutes to allow it to firm up and develop flavors.
6. Serve: Once chilled, serve the chocolate avocado pudding topped with fresh berries, sliced bananas, chopped nuts, or shredded coconut if desired.

Tips:

- Avocado ripeness: Use ripe avocados for the best texture and flavor. They should be soft to the touch but not overly mushy.
- Sweetness: Adjust the amount of maple syrup or honey based on your preference for sweetness. You can also use a sugar substitute like stevia or agave syrup.
- Storage: Store leftover pudding in an airtight container in the refrigerator for up to 2 days. Avocado-based puddings can oxidize and change color slightly over time, but they are still safe to eat.

This chocolate avocado pudding is a decadent yet healthy dessert option, rich in healthy fats from avocados and antioxidants from cocoa powder. It's perfect for satisfying chocolate cravings while offering a nutritious twist. Enjoy this creamy and indulgent treat guilt-free!

Almond Joy Energy Bites

Ingredients:

- 1 cup old-fashioned rolled oats
- 1/2 cup almond butter (or any nut butter of your choice)
- 1/4 cup honey or maple syrup
- 1/4 cup shredded coconut (unsweetened)
- 1/4 cup chopped almonds
- 1/4 cup mini chocolate chips (dark or semi-sweet)
- 1 teaspoon vanilla extract
- Pinch of salt

Optional Coating:

- Additional shredded coconut, for rolling
- Melted chocolate, for drizzling

Instructions:

1. Mix ingredients: In a large bowl, combine the rolled oats, almond butter, honey or maple syrup, shredded coconut, chopped almonds, mini chocolate chips, vanilla extract, and a pinch of salt. Stir until well combined.
2. Chill mixture: Cover the bowl and place it in the refrigerator for 30 minutes to 1 hour. Chilling will make the mixture easier to roll into balls.
3. Form balls: Once chilled, take about a tablespoon of the mixture and roll it into a ball between your palms. Repeat with the remaining mixture to form energy bites.
4. Optional coating: If desired, roll the energy bites in additional shredded coconut for an extra layer of coconut flavor and texture. Alternatively, drizzle melted chocolate over the energy bites for a chocolate coating.
5. Chill: Place the energy bites on a baking sheet lined with parchment paper and chill in the refrigerator for another 30 minutes to firm up.
6. Serve and store: Once chilled, transfer the energy bites to an airtight container and store them in the refrigerator for up to 1 week.

Tips:

- Nut butter: If you prefer a nut-free option, you can use sunflower seed butter or tahini instead of almond butter.
- Sweetener: Adjust the amount of honey or maple syrup based on your preferred level of sweetness.
- Variations: Feel free to add other mix-ins like chia seeds, dried fruit, or a scoop of protein powder for additional nutrients.

These Almond Joy energy bites are perfect for a quick snack on the go, providing a boost of energy and satisfying your sweet cravings in a healthier way. Enjoy these delicious bites whenever you need a nutritious pick-me-up!

Mocha Hazelnut Mousse

Ingredients:

- 1 cup heavy cream
- 1/2 cup Nutella or other chocolate hazelnut spread
- 2 tablespoons cocoa powder (unsweetened)
- 2 tablespoons instant coffee or espresso powder
- 1/4 cup powdered sugar (adjust to taste)
- 1 teaspoon vanilla extract
- Optional garnish: Whipped cream, chocolate shavings, chopped hazelnuts

Instructions:

1. Prepare the coffee mixture:
    - In a small bowl, dissolve the instant coffee or espresso powder in 2 tablespoons of hot water. Set aside to cool.
2. Whip the cream:
    - In a large mixing bowl, beat the heavy cream until soft peaks form.
3. Mix in chocolate hazelnut spread and cocoa powder:
    - Add the Nutella (or chocolate hazelnut spread) and cocoa powder to the whipped cream. Beat until well combined and smooth.
4. Add coffee mixture and vanilla:
    - Pour in the cooled coffee mixture and vanilla extract. Beat again until everything is evenly incorporated.
5. Sweeten to taste:
    - Taste the mousse and add powdered sugar as needed to reach your desired level of sweetness. Beat until smooth.
6. Chill:
    - Cover the bowl with plastic wrap or transfer the mousse into serving glasses or bowls. Refrigerate for at least 1 hour to allow the flavors to meld and the mousse to set.
7. Serve:
    - Before serving, top the mocha hazelnut mousse with whipped cream, chocolate shavings, or chopped hazelnuts for extra flavor and texture.

Tips:

- Nutella substitution: If you prefer a homemade version or a different brand of chocolate hazelnut spread, feel free to use it in place of Nutella.
- Coffee intensity: Adjust the amount of instant coffee or espresso powder according to your preference for a stronger or milder coffee flavor.
- Texture: For a lighter mousse, fold in whipped cream gently instead of beating it into the mixture.

This mocha hazelnut mousse is perfect for special occasions or whenever you crave a luxurious dessert with the classic combination of chocolate and hazelnut flavors. Enjoy the creamy, airy texture and the delightful coffee undertones in every spoonful!

Mango Coconut Rice Pudding

Ingredients:

- 1 cup jasmine rice (or any medium-grain rice)
- 2 cups water
- 1 can (13.5 oz) coconut milk (full fat)
- 1/4 cup granulated sugar (adjust to taste)
- 1/4 teaspoon salt
- 1 ripe mango, peeled and diced
- 1/2 teaspoon vanilla extract
- Optional garnish: Toasted coconut flakes, mango slices, mint leaves

Instructions:

1. Cook the rice:
   - Rinse the jasmine rice under cold water until the water runs clear. In a medium saucepan, bring 2 cups of water to a boil. Add the rinsed rice, reduce heat to low, cover, and simmer for about 15-20 minutes, or until the rice is cooked and water is absorbed. Remove from heat and let it cool slightly.
2. Prepare the coconut milk mixture:
   - In another saucepan, combine the coconut milk, granulated sugar, and salt. Heat over medium heat, stirring occasionally, until the sugar is dissolved and the mixture is smooth and creamy. Stir in the vanilla extract.
3. Combine rice and coconut mixture:
   - Add the cooked rice to the coconut milk mixture, stirring gently to combine. Cook over low heat for another 5-10 minutes, stirring occasionally, until the pudding thickens to your desired consistency. Remove from heat and let it cool slightly.
4. Add mango:
   - Gently fold in the diced mango into the rice pudding mixture. Reserve a few mango pieces for garnish if desired.
5. Chill and serve:
   - Transfer the mango coconut rice pudding to serving bowls or glasses. Cover and refrigerate for at least 2 hours, or until chilled.
6. Garnish and serve:
   - Before serving, garnish with toasted coconut flakes, mango slices, and mint leaves if desired. Serve chilled.

Tips:

- Ripe mango: Use a ripe mango for the best flavor and sweetness. You can also use frozen mango chunks that have been thawed.
- Sweetness: Adjust the amount of sugar according to your preference and the sweetness of the mango.

- Texture: If you prefer a smoother pudding, blend half of the mango with the coconut milk mixture before combining with the rice.

This mango coconut rice pudding is creamy, aromatic, and bursting with tropical flavors. It's a perfect dessert for hot days or anytime you want to indulge in a refreshing and exotic treat. Enjoy the creamy coconut milk base complemented by the sweetness of ripe mango!

Blackberry Lime Sorbet

Ingredients:

- 4 cups fresh or frozen blackberries
- 1 cup granulated sugar
- 1/2 cup water
- Zest and juice of 2 limes (about 1/4 cup lime juice)
- Pinch of salt

Instructions:

1. Prepare the blackberries:
    - If using fresh blackberries, rinse them under cold water and remove any stems. If using frozen blackberries, thaw them slightly.
2. Make the simple syrup:
    - In a small saucepan, combine the granulated sugar and water. Heat over medium heat, stirring occasionally, until the sugar is completely dissolved. Remove from heat and let it cool slightly.
3. Blend blackberries and lime:
    - In a blender or food processor, combine the blackberries, lime zest, lime juice, and pinch of salt. Blend until smooth.
4. Strain the mixture (optional):
    - For a smoother sorbet, strain the blackberry mixture through a fine-mesh sieve to remove the seeds. Press down with a spoon to extract as much liquid as possible.
5. Combine ingredients:
    - Stir the cooled simple syrup into the blackberry mixture. Taste and adjust sweetness by adding more sugar if desired (keep in mind that freezing will reduce sweetness slightly).
6. Chill the mixture:
    - Cover the mixture and refrigerate for at least 1 hour, or until thoroughly chilled.
7. Churn the sorbet:
    - Pour the chilled blackberry mixture into an ice cream maker and churn according to the manufacturer's instructions, typically 20-30 minutes, or until it reaches a soft-serve consistency.
8. Freeze the sorbet:
    - Transfer the sorbet to a freezer-safe container. Cover tightly with plastic wrap or a lid and freeze for at least 4 hours, or until firm.
9. Serve:
    - Scoop the blackberry lime sorbet into bowls or cones. Garnish with fresh blackberries, mint leaves, or a wedge of lime if desired. Enjoy immediately!

Tips:

- Texture: If you prefer a smoother sorbet, strain the blackberry mixture after blending to remove the seeds.
- Sweetness: Adjust the amount of sugar based on the sweetness of your blackberries and personal preference.
- Storage: Store any leftover sorbet in an airtight container in the freezer for up to a few weeks. Allow it to soften slightly at room temperature before scooping.

This blackberry lime sorbet is a delightful and vibrant dessert, perfect for hot summer days or any time you crave a fruity and refreshing treat. Enjoy the bright flavors of blackberries and lime in every spoonful!

Pumpkin Pie Bites

Ingredients:

- 1 cup pumpkin puree (canned or homemade)
- 1/4 cup maple syrup or honey
- 1 teaspoon vanilla extract
- 1 teaspoon ground cinnamon
- 1/2 teaspoon ground ginger
- 1/4 teaspoon ground nutmeg
- 1/4 teaspoon ground cloves
- Pinch of salt
- 1/2 cup coconut cream (or full-fat canned coconut milk, chilled)
- 1/4 cup coconut flour
- 1/4 cup almond flour
- Optional: 1/4 cup chopped pecans or walnuts for garnish

Instructions:

1. Prepare the pumpkin filling:
    - In a mixing bowl, combine the pumpkin puree, maple syrup or honey, vanilla extract, ground cinnamon, ground ginger, ground nutmeg, ground cloves, and a pinch of salt. Mix until smooth and well combined. Set aside.
2. Make the coconut cream topping:
    - In a separate mixing bowl, scoop out the thickened coconut cream from the top of a chilled can of coconut milk (or use coconut cream directly). Whip it using a hand mixer or whisk until fluffy and peaks form.
3. Combine flours and form dough:
    - In another bowl, mix together the coconut flour and almond flour. Add the flour mixture to the pumpkin filling gradually, stirring until you achieve a dough-like consistency that holds together.
4. Shape the pumpkin pie bites:
    - Using your hands, roll the dough into small balls, about 1 to 1.5 inches in diameter, and place them on a baking sheet lined with parchment paper.
5. Top with coconut cream and nuts:
    - Use a small spoon or piping bag to add a dollop of whipped coconut cream on top of each pumpkin pie bite. Optionally, sprinkle chopped pecans or walnuts on top for garnish.
6. Chill and serve:
    - Place the pumpkin pie bites in the refrigerator to chill for at least 30 minutes before serving. This helps them firm up and enhances the flavors.
7. Enjoy:
    - Serve chilled and enjoy these delightful pumpkin pie bites as a tasty and healthier dessert option!

Tips:

- Texture: Adjust the amount of coconut flour and almond flour as needed to achieve a dough consistency that is easy to shape.
- Sweetness: Taste the pumpkin filling before shaping the bites and adjust the sweetness by adding more maple syrup or honey if desired.
- Variations: Feel free to customize these bites by adding a sprinkle of cinnamon or nutmeg on top of the coconut cream, or drizzle with melted dark chocolate for an extra decadent touch.

These pumpkin pie bites are a delicious way to enjoy the flavors of pumpkin pie in a convenient and bite-sized form. They're perfect for fall festivities or any time you're craving a taste of autumn!

Caramelized Banana Slices

Ingredients:

- 2 ripe but firm bananas
- 2 tablespoons unsalted butter
- 2 tablespoons brown sugar (adjust to taste)
- 1/2 teaspoon ground cinnamon (optional)
- Pinch of salt

Instructions:

1. Prepare the bananas:
   - Peel the bananas and slice them into rounds, about 1/4 to 1/2 inch thick.
2. Heat the butter:
   - In a large skillet or frying pan, melt the butter over medium heat.
3. Caramelize the bananas:
   - Once the butter is melted and bubbling, add the banana slices to the skillet in a single layer. Cook for about 1-2 minutes on each side, or until the bananas start to caramelize and turn golden brown.
4. Add sugar and cinnamon:
   - Sprinkle the brown sugar and ground cinnamon (if using) evenly over the banana slices. Gently stir to coat the bananas with the caramelized sugar mixture.
5. Cook until caramelized:
   - Continue to cook the banana slices, stirring occasionally, for another 1-2 minutes or until the sugar has melted and caramelized, forming a golden-brown coating on the bananas.
6. Remove from heat:
   - Remove the skillet from heat and let the caramelized banana slices cool slightly before serving.
7. Serve:
   - Serve the caramelized banana slices warm as a topping for pancakes, waffles, yogurt, or ice cream. They can also be used as a filling for crepes or enjoyed on their own as a delicious snack.

Tips:

- Banana ripeness: Use ripe but firm bananas for best results. Overripe bananas may become too mushy during cooking.
- Adjust sweetness: Adjust the amount of brown sugar according to your preference and the sweetness of your bananas.
- Variations: For an extra touch of flavor, you can add a splash of vanilla extract or a pinch of nutmeg along with the cinnamon.

Caramelized banana slices are quick and easy to make, and they add a wonderful sweet and caramelized flavor to various dishes and desserts. Enjoy their warm, gooey goodness any time you crave a comforting and indulgent treat!

Hazelnut Flourless Cake

Ingredients:

- 1 cup hazelnuts, toasted and skins removed
- 1 cup granulated sugar
- 1/2 cup unsalted butter, melted
- 4 large eggs, separated
- 1 teaspoon vanilla extract
- 1/4 teaspoon salt
- Optional: Powdered sugar, whipped cream, or berries for serving

Instructions:

1. Prepare the hazelnuts:
   - Preheat your oven to 350°F (175°C). Spread the hazelnuts evenly on a baking sheet and toast them in the oven for about 10-12 minutes, or until fragrant and lightly golden. Remove from the oven and let them cool slightly. Rub the hazelnuts in a clean kitchen towel to remove the skins.
2. Grind hazelnuts:
   - In a food processor, grind the toasted hazelnuts with 1/4 cup of granulated sugar until finely ground. Be careful not to over-process, or the hazelnuts may release their oils and become too sticky.
3. Prepare the batter:
   - In a large mixing bowl, whisk together the melted butter and remaining 3/4 cup of granulated sugar until well combined. Add the egg yolks one at a time, beating well after each addition. Stir in the vanilla extract.
4. Combine with hazelnuts:
   - Gently fold the ground hazelnuts into the butter and sugar mixture until evenly incorporated.
5. Whip egg whites:
   - In a separate clean mixing bowl, using an electric mixer, beat the egg whites and salt until stiff peaks form.
6. Fold in egg whites:
   - Carefully fold the whipped egg whites into the hazelnut mixture in two additions, using a spatula. Take care not to deflate the egg whites completely; the batter should be light and airy.
7. Bake the cake:
   - Pour the batter into a greased 9-inch round cake pan lined with parchment paper. Smooth the top with a spatula. Bake in the preheated oven for 30-35 minutes, or until the top is golden brown and a toothpick inserted into the center comes out clean.
8. Cool and serve:

- Allow the cake to cool in the pan for about 10 minutes before transferring it to a wire rack to cool completely. Dust with powdered sugar before serving if desired. Serve slices of hazelnut flourless cake with whipped cream or fresh berries.

Tips:

- Toasting hazelnuts: Toasting the hazelnuts enhances their flavor. Keep an eye on them as they toast quickly.
- Ground hazelnuts: It's essential to grind the hazelnuts finely, but be cautious not to turn them into hazelnut butter.
- Storage: Store leftovers in an airtight container at room temperature for up to 2 days, or refrigerate for longer storage.

This hazelnut flourless cake is dense, moist, and full of nutty flavor, making it a perfect gluten-free dessert option. Enjoy its rich texture and delightful hazelnut taste with every bite!

Orange Cardamom Cookies

Ingredients:

- 1 cup unsalted butter, softened
- 1 cup granulated sugar
- Zest of 2 oranges
- 2 tablespoons freshly squeezed orange juice
- 2 teaspoons ground cardamom
- 2 teaspoons vanilla extract
- 2 cups all-purpose flour
- 1/2 teaspoon baking powder
- 1/4 teaspoon salt
- Optional: Powdered sugar for dusting

Instructions:

1. Preheat the oven:
    - Preheat your oven to 350°F (175°C). Line baking sheets with parchment paper or silicone baking mats.
2. Cream butter and sugar:
    - In a large mixing bowl, cream together the softened butter and granulated sugar until light and fluffy.
3. Add orange zest and juice:
    - Mix in the orange zest, freshly squeezed orange juice, ground cardamom, and vanilla extract until well combined.
4. Combine dry ingredients:
    - In a separate bowl, whisk together the flour, baking powder, and salt.
5. Mix wet and dry ingredients:
    - Gradually add the dry ingredients to the wet ingredients, mixing until a dough forms. If the dough is too sticky, you can refrigerate it for about 30 minutes to firm up.
6. Form cookies:
    - Roll tablespoon-sized portions of dough into balls and place them on the prepared baking sheets, spacing them about 2 inches apart. Flatten each ball slightly with the palm of your hand or the bottom of a glass.
7. Bake the cookies:
    - Bake in the preheated oven for 12-15 minutes, or until the edges are lightly golden. The tops of the cookies should be set but still soft.
8. Cool and dust with powdered sugar:
    - Allow the cookies to cool on the baking sheets for a few minutes before transferring them to a wire rack to cool completely. Dust with powdered sugar before serving if desired.
9. Store:

- Store the cookies in an airtight container at room temperature for up to one week.

Tips:

- Fresh ingredients: Use freshly grated orange zest and juice for the best citrus flavor.
- Cardamom: Adjust the amount of ground cardamom according to your preference for spice intensity.
- Variations: For added texture, you can mix in chopped nuts or dried fruit such as cranberries or chopped apricots.

These orange cardamom cookies are perfect for tea time, dessert, or as a homemade gift. Enjoy the aromatic blend of orange and cardamom in every delicious bite!

Berry Compote with Yogurt

Ingredients:

- 2 cups mixed berries (such as strawberries, blueberries, raspberries, blackberries)
- 1/4 cup granulated sugar (adjust to taste)
- 1 tablespoon fresh lemon juice
- 1 teaspoon cornstarch (optional, for thickening)
- 2 cups Greek yogurt or plain yogurt
- Honey or maple syrup (optional, for sweetening yogurt)
- Fresh mint leaves, for garnish (optional)

Instructions:

1. Prepare the berries:
    - Rinse the berries under cold water and drain well. If using strawberries, hull and slice them into smaller pieces if desired.
2. Make the berry compote:
    - In a medium saucepan, combine the mixed berries, granulated sugar, and fresh lemon juice. Stir gently to combine.
3. Cook the compote:
    - Heat the berry mixture over medium heat, stirring occasionally, until the berries release their juices and the sugar is dissolved. If you prefer a thicker compote, mix 1 teaspoon of cornstarch with 1 tablespoon of water and add it to the berry mixture. Cook for an additional 1-2 minutes, stirring constantly, until the mixture thickens slightly. Remove from heat and let it cool slightly.
4. Prepare the yogurt:
    - In a separate bowl, mix the Greek yogurt or plain yogurt with honey or maple syrup to sweeten, if desired.
5. Assemble:
    - Spoon the yogurt into serving bowls or glasses. Top with the warm or cooled berry compote.
6. Garnish and serve:
    - Garnish with fresh mint leaves if desired. Serve the berry compote with yogurt immediately, while the compote is still warm, or refrigerate both components separately and assemble just before serving.

Tips:

- Frozen berries: If using frozen berries, thaw them before cooking. You can also use a combination of fresh and frozen berries.
- Sweetness: Adjust the amount of sugar in the compote according to the sweetness of the berries and your personal preference.

- Variations: Add a splash of vanilla extract or a sprinkle of cinnamon to the yogurt for extra flavor.

This berry compote with yogurt makes for a delicious breakfast, brunch, or dessert option. The contrast between the warm or chilled compote and the creamy yogurt is both refreshing and satisfying. Enjoy this simple yet flavorful dish any time of day!

Pistachio Crusted Yogurt Bars

Ingredients:

- 2 cups plain Greek yogurt (or regular yogurt, strained if desired)
- 1/4 cup honey or maple syrup (adjust to taste)
- 1 teaspoon vanilla extract
- 1 cup shelled pistachios, finely chopped or ground
- 1/4 cup coconut oil, melted
- Pinch of salt

Instructions:

1. Prepare the yogurt mixture:
    - In a mixing bowl, combine the Greek yogurt, honey or maple syrup, and vanilla extract. Mix until smooth and well combined. Taste and adjust sweetness if necessary.
2. Prepare the pistachio crust:
    - In a separate bowl, mix together the finely chopped or ground pistachios, melted coconut oil, and a pinch of salt. Stir until the mixture resembles coarse crumbs and holds together when pressed.
3. Assemble the bars:
    - Line an 8x8 inch baking dish with parchment paper or foil, leaving some overhang for easy removal later. Spread half of the pistachio mixture evenly into the bottom of the dish, pressing down firmly to form a crust.
    - Spoon the yogurt mixture over the pistachio crust, spreading it out evenly with a spatula.
    - Sprinkle the remaining pistachio mixture over the top of the yogurt layer, pressing down gently to adhere.
4. Chill and set:
    - Place the baking dish in the refrigerator and chill for at least 4 hours, or until the bars are firm and set.
5. Slice and serve:
    - Once chilled, lift the bars out of the baking dish using the parchment paper or foil overhang. Cut into squares or bars using a sharp knife.
6. Optional garnish:
    - Garnish with additional chopped pistachios or a drizzle of honey before serving, if desired.
7. Storage:
    - Store the pistachio crusted yogurt bars in an airtight container in the refrigerator for up to 5 days. They can also be frozen for longer storage.

Tips:

- Yogurt consistency: For a thicker yogurt layer, you can strain the Greek yogurt using cheesecloth or a fine-mesh sieve over a bowl to remove excess liquid.
- Variations: Feel free to add a sprinkle of cinnamon or a dash of cardamom to the yogurt mixture for additional flavor.
- Nut allergies: If you have nut allergies or prefer a different texture, you can substitute the pistachios with finely chopped oats or granola for the crust.

These pistachio crusted yogurt bars are creamy, crunchy, and packed with protein, making them a satisfying and nutritious snack or dessert option. Enjoy their refreshing flavor and delightful texture with every bite!

Chocolate Covered Strawberries

Ingredients:

- Fresh strawberries, rinsed and dried thoroughly
- 6 ounces (about 1 cup) of chocolate chips or chopped chocolate (dark, milk, or white)
- 1 tablespoon coconut oil or vegetable shortening (optional, for smoother chocolate)
- Optional toppings: Chopped nuts, shredded coconut, sprinkles, sea salt

Instructions:

1. Prepare the strawberries:
    - Rinse the strawberries under cold water and pat them dry completely with paper towels. Make sure they are completely dry before dipping in chocolate to prevent the chocolate from seizing.
2. Melt the chocolate:
    - In a microwave-safe bowl or using a double boiler, melt the chocolate chips or chopped chocolate until smooth. If using the microwave, heat in 30-second intervals, stirring in between each interval until melted. If using a double boiler, stir constantly until melted.
3. Add coconut oil (optional):
    - For a smoother and shinier chocolate coating, stir in 1 tablespoon of coconut oil or vegetable shortening into the melted chocolate until fully incorporated.
4. Dip the strawberries:
    - Hold each strawberry by the stem (or use a toothpick inserted into the stem end) and dip it into the melted chocolate, swirling to coat evenly. Allow excess chocolate to drip back into the bowl.
5. Place on parchment paper:
    - Place the chocolate-covered strawberries on a parchment paper-lined baking sheet or plate. This will prevent them from sticking and make cleanup easier.
6. Optional toppings:
    - While the chocolate is still wet, sprinkle your choice of toppings such as chopped nuts, shredded coconut, sprinkles, or a pinch of sea salt over the strawberries.
7. Set and chill:
    - Once all strawberries are dipped and decorated, refrigerate them for about 30 minutes or until the chocolate sets completely.
8. Serve and enjoy:
    - Arrange the chocolate covered strawberries on a serving platter and serve immediately, or store them in the refrigerator until ready to serve.

Tips:

- Quality chocolate: Use high-quality chocolate for the best taste and texture. Dark chocolate complements the sweetness of strawberries well, but you can also use milk or white chocolate according to your preference.
- Decorating: Experiment with different toppings and drizzles for variety. You can also drizzle melted white or dark chocolate over the dipped strawberries for an added decorative touch.
- Storing: Chocolate covered strawberries are best enjoyed the same day they are made but can be stored in an airtight container in the refrigerator for up to 2 days. However, they may lose their crispness over time.

These chocolate covered strawberries are perfect for special occasions, romantic gestures, or as a sweet treat any time of year. Enjoy the combination of juicy strawberries and rich chocolate in every delightful bite!

Maple Pecan Blondies

Ingredients:

- 1/2 cup unsalted butter, melted
- 1 cup light brown sugar, packed
- 1/4 cup maple syrup
- 1 large egg
- 1 teaspoon vanilla extract
- 1 cup all-purpose flour
- 1/2 teaspoon baking powder
- 1/4 teaspoon salt
- 1/2 cup chopped pecans
- Optional: Sea salt flakes for sprinkling on top

Instructions:

1. Preheat your oven:
    - Preheat the oven to 350°F (175°C). Grease and line an 8x8-inch baking pan with parchment paper, leaving an overhang for easy removal.
2. Prepare the wet ingredients:
    - In a large mixing bowl, whisk together the melted butter, brown sugar, and maple syrup until smooth.
3. Add the egg and vanilla:
    - Beat in the egg and vanilla extract until well combined.
4. Combine the dry ingredients:
    - In a separate bowl, whisk together the flour, baking powder, and salt.
5. Mix the batter:
    - Gradually add the dry ingredients to the wet ingredients, stirring until just combined. Be careful not to overmix.
6. Fold in the pecans:
    - Gently fold in the chopped pecans until evenly distributed throughout the batter.
7. Bake the blondies:
    - Pour the batter into the prepared baking pan, spreading it out evenly with a spatula. Smooth the top.
8. Bake in the preheated oven:
    - Bake for 20-25 minutes, or until the top is golden brown and a toothpick inserted into the center comes out with a few moist crumbs. Be careful not to overbake to keep the blondies moist.
9. Cool and slice:
    - Remove the blondies from the oven and allow them to cool completely in the pan on a wire rack. Once cooled, lift them out using the parchment paper overhang and transfer to a cutting board.
10. Optional: Sprinkle with sea salt:

- If desired, sprinkle the top of the blondies with sea salt flakes for a sweet-salty contrast.
11. Slice into squares:
    - Cut into squares or bars using a sharp knife. Enjoy these maple pecan blondies as a delicious dessert or snack!

Tips:

- Maple syrup: Use pure maple syrup for the best flavor. You can adjust the amount to taste depending on how pronounced you want the maple flavor to be.
- Pecans: Toast the pecans before chopping for a richer flavor. Alternatively, you can substitute with other nuts like walnuts or almonds.
- Storage: Store leftover blondies in an airtight container at room temperature for up to 3 days, or refrigerate for longer storage.

These maple pecan blondies are chewy, buttery, and packed with nutty goodness, making them a perfect treat for any occasion. Enjoy the comforting flavors of maple and pecans in every bite!

Tiramisu Cups

Ingredients:

- 1 cup heavy cream
- 1/4 cup powdered sugar
- 1 teaspoon vanilla extract
- 8 ounces mascarpone cheese, softened
- 1/2 cup strong brewed coffee or espresso, cooled
- 2 tablespoons coffee liqueur (such as Kahlua), optional
- 24-30 ladyfinger cookies (savoiardi)
- Cocoa powder, for dusting

Instructions:

1. Prepare the whipped cream:
   - In a large mixing bowl, whip the heavy cream, powdered sugar, and vanilla extract together until stiff peaks form. Set aside.
2. Prepare the mascarpone mixture:
   - In another bowl, whisk the mascarpone cheese until smooth and creamy. Gradually fold in about half of the whipped cream mixture until well combined and smooth. Set the remaining whipped cream aside for later use.
3. Combine coffee mixture:
   - In a shallow bowl, mix the cooled brewed coffee or espresso with the coffee liqueur (if using).
4. Assemble the tiramisu cups:
   - Dip each ladyfinger cookie briefly into the coffee mixture, ensuring they are soaked but not overly saturated. Break them in half if needed to fit into your serving cups.
   - Place a layer of soaked ladyfingers at the bottom of each serving cup.
   - Spoon a layer of the mascarpone mixture over the ladyfingers, spreading it evenly.
   - Repeat with another layer of soaked ladyfingers followed by another layer of mascarpone mixture until you reach the top of each cup, finishing with a layer of the mascarpone mixture.
5. Chill:
   - Cover the tiramisu cups with plastic wrap and refrigerate for at least 2 hours, or overnight, to allow the flavors to meld and the dessert to set.
6. Serve:
   - Before serving, top each tiramisu cup with a dollop of the reserved whipped cream.
7. Dust with cocoa powder:
   - Using a fine-mesh sieve, dust the tops of the tiramisu cups with cocoa powder just before serving.

8. Optional garnish:
    - Garnish with chocolate shavings, cocoa nibs, or a chocolate-covered coffee bean for an extra touch.

Tips:

- Ladyfinger alternatives: If you can't find ladyfinger cookies, you can use sponge cake or even graham crackers as a substitute.
- Coffee liqueur: The coffee liqueur adds extra flavor, but you can omit it if you prefer a non-alcoholic version.
- Make ahead: Tiramisu cups can be assembled ahead of time and stored in the refrigerator overnight, making them a convenient dessert option for entertaining.

These tiramisu cups are creamy, decadent, and full of coffee and mascarpone flavors, making them a perfect individual dessert for any occasion. Enjoy the indulgent taste of classic Italian tiramisu in a convenient cup format!

Key Lime Pie Jars

Ingredients:

For the crust:

- 1 1/2 cups graham cracker crumbs (about 10-12 graham crackers)
- 6 tablespoons unsalted butter, melted
- 3 tablespoons granulated sugar

For the filling:

- 14 ounces (1 can) sweetened condensed milk
- 1/2 cup key lime juice (freshly squeezed if possible)
- Zest of 2 limes (optional, for extra flavor)
- 1 cup heavy cream
- 2 tablespoons powdered sugar
- Lime slices or zest, for garnish (optional)

Instructions:

1. Prepare the crust:
    - In a medium bowl, combine the graham cracker crumbs, melted butter, and granulated sugar until well mixed and crumbly.
    - Press the crumb mixture evenly into the bottoms of individual serving jars or glasses. You can use the bottom of a small glass or a spoon to press the crumbs firmly.
2. Make the filling:
    - In a separate bowl, whisk together the sweetened condensed milk, key lime juice, and lime zest (if using) until smooth and well combined.
3. Fill the jars:
    - Spoon the key lime filling evenly over the graham cracker crust in each jar, leaving a little space at the top for the whipped cream.
4. Chill:
    - Cover the jars with plastic wrap and refrigerate for at least 2 hours, or until the filling is set.
5. Prepare the whipped cream:
    - In a mixing bowl, whip the heavy cream and powdered sugar together until stiff peaks form.
6. Top the jars:
    - Spoon or pipe the whipped cream onto the top of each key lime pie jar.
7. Garnish:
    - Garnish with lime slices or zest on top, if desired.
8. Serve:
    - Serve chilled and enjoy these delicious individual key lime pie jars!

Tips:

- Key lime juice: Freshly squeezed key lime juice is preferred for the best flavor, but bottled key lime juice works as well.
- Make ahead: You can prepare these key lime pie jars a day ahead of time and keep them refrigerated until ready to serve.
- Variations: For a twist, you can add a layer of whipped cream cheese or incorporate toasted coconut into the graham cracker crust.

These key lime pie jars are a refreshing and tangy dessert that captures the essence of a classic key lime pie in a convenient individual serving. They're perfect for parties, picnics, or simply as a delightful treat to enjoy at home!

Cacao Nib Rice Crispy Treats

Ingredients:

- 4 cups crispy rice cereal
- 4 cups mini marshmallows
- 3 tablespoons unsalted butter
- 1/2 cup cacao nibs
- 1/2 teaspoon vanilla extract
- Pinch of salt

Instructions:

1. Prepare a baking dish:
   - Grease a 9x13-inch baking dish with butter or non-stick cooking spray. Set aside.
2. Melt the marshmallows and butter:
   - In a large saucepan, melt the butter over medium heat. Add the mini marshmallows and stir constantly until they are completely melted and smooth.
3. Add vanilla and salt:
   - Stir in the vanilla extract and a pinch of salt to the marshmallow mixture. Mix until well combined.
4. Combine with cereal and cacao nibs:
   - Remove the saucepan from the heat. Quickly add the crispy rice cereal and cacao nibs to the marshmallow mixture. Stir until the cereal and cacao nibs are evenly coated with the marshmallow mixture.
5. Press into the baking dish:
   - Transfer the mixture into the prepared baking dish. Use a buttered spatula or parchment paper to press the mixture evenly into the dish, smoothing the top.
6. Let cool and set:
   - Allow the rice crispy treats to cool at room temperature for about 30 minutes, or until completely set.
7. Cut into squares:
   - Once cooled and set, cut the treats into squares or bars using a sharp knife.
8. Serve:
   - Serve the cacao nib rice crispy treats immediately, or store them in an airtight container at room temperature for up to 3 days.

Tips:

- Cacao nibs: Cacao nibs add a crunchy texture and a rich chocolate flavor. If you prefer a sweeter treat, you can use chocolate chips instead.
- Variations: For a twist, you can drizzle melted chocolate over the top of the rice crispy treats or sprinkle additional cacao nibs before they completely set.

- Storage: Keep the treats in an airtight container at room temperature. If it's warm, you may want to store them in the refrigerator to keep them from becoming too soft.

These cacao nib rice crispy treats are perfect for satisfying a sweet craving with a touch of chocolatey goodness and crunchiness from the cacao nibs. Enjoy making and indulging in these delicious treats!

Peach Ginger Sorbet

Ingredients:

- 4 ripe peaches, peeled, pitted, and chopped (about 4 cups)
- 1/2 cup granulated sugar
- 1/4 cup water
- 1 tablespoon fresh ginger, grated
- 1 tablespoon lemon juice
- Pinch of salt

Instructions:

1. Prepare the peaches:
   - Peel, pit, and chop the ripe peaches. You should have about 4 cups of chopped peaches.
2. Make the ginger syrup:
   - In a small saucepan, combine the granulated sugar, water, grated ginger, lemon juice, and a pinch of salt. Bring to a simmer over medium heat, stirring occasionally, until the sugar is completely dissolved. Remove from heat and let the ginger syrup cool to room temperature.
3. Blend the peaches:
   - In a blender or food processor, puree the chopped peaches until smooth.
4. Combine peach puree and ginger syrup:
   - Pour the ginger syrup through a fine-mesh sieve into the peach puree to remove the grated ginger solids. Stir to combine the peach puree with the ginger syrup.
5. Chill the mixture:
   - Cover the peach ginger mixture and refrigerate until well chilled, preferably for at least 2 hours or overnight.
6. Churn the sorbet:
   - Pour the chilled peach ginger mixture into an ice cream maker and churn according to the manufacturer's instructions until it reaches a soft-serve consistency.
7. Freeze the sorbet:
   - Transfer the churned sorbet into a freezer-safe container. Cover with parchment paper or plastic wrap directly on the surface of the sorbet to prevent ice crystals from forming. Freeze for at least 4 hours or until firm.
8. Serve:
   - Scoop the peach ginger sorbet into bowls or cones and enjoy its refreshing flavor!

Tips:

- Ripe peaches: Use ripe and flavorful peaches for the best taste. If peaches are not in season, you can use frozen peaches that have been thawed.
- Ginger intensity: Adjust the amount of grated ginger according to your preference for a stronger or milder ginger flavor.
- Storage: Store any leftover sorbet in an airtight container in the freezer. Let it soften slightly at room temperature for a few minutes before scooping and serving.

This peach ginger sorbet is a perfect summer dessert, offering a balance of sweet peach with a subtle kick of ginger. It's light, refreshing, and sure to be a hit at any gathering or as a treat on a warm day!

Almond Flour Shortbread

Ingredients:

- 1 cup almond flour
- 2 tablespoons coconut flour (optional, for texture)
- 1/4 cup powdered sugar (or sweetener of choice, adjust to taste)
- 1/4 teaspoon salt
- 6 tablespoons unsalted butter, softened
- 1/2 teaspoon vanilla extract (optional)

Instructions:

1. Preheat oven and prepare baking sheet:
   - Preheat your oven to 325°F (160°C). Line a baking sheet with parchment paper or silicone baking mat.
2. Mix dry ingredients:
   - In a mixing bowl, combine almond flour, coconut flour (if using), powdered sugar, and salt. Stir until well combined.
3. Add butter and vanilla:
   - Add the softened butter and vanilla extract to the dry ingredients. Use a fork or pastry cutter to cut the butter into the flour mixture until it resembles coarse crumbs and begins to hold together.
4. Form the dough:
   - Use your hands to bring the dough together into a ball. If the dough seems too crumbly, you can add a teaspoon of water or almond milk to help bind it together.
5. Shape the shortbread:
   - Place the dough between two sheets of parchment paper or plastic wrap. Roll out the dough to about 1/4-inch thickness. Alternatively, you can press the dough evenly into an 8x8-inch square baking pan lined with parchment paper.
6. Cut into shapes:
   - Use a cookie cutter to cut the dough into desired shapes (such as rounds or squares). Alternatively, you can cut the dough into bars if using a baking pan.
7. Bake:
   - Carefully transfer the cut-out cookies to the prepared baking sheet. Place them about 1 inch apart. Prick each cookie with a fork to create a decorative pattern (optional).
   - Bake in the preheated oven for 12-15 minutes, or until the edges are lightly golden brown. The baking time may vary depending on the thickness of your cookies.
8. Cool and serve:
   - Remove from the oven and let the cookies cool on the baking sheet for 5 minutes. Then transfer them to a wire rack to cool completely.
9. Optional: Dip in chocolate (if desired):

- For an extra touch, you can dip cooled almond flour shortbread cookies halfway into melted chocolate and let them set on parchment paper.
10. Store:
    - Store the almond flour shortbread cookies in an airtight container at room temperature for up to 5 days. They can also be stored in the refrigerator for longer freshness.

Tips:

- Powdered sugar: If you prefer a sweeter shortbread, you can increase the amount of powdered sugar to suit your taste.
- Flavor variations: Add a teaspoon of lemon zest or almond extract for additional flavor.
- Gluten-free baking: Ensure all your ingredients are certified gluten-free if you have gluten allergies or sensitivities.

These almond flour shortbread cookies are buttery, crumbly, and perfect for enjoying with a cup of tea or coffee. They make a delightful treat for anyone looking to enjoy gluten-free baking with a nutty twist!

Vegan Chocolate Truffles

Ingredients:

- 8 ounces (about 1 1/3 cups) dairy-free dark chocolate, finely chopped
- 1/2 cup full-fat coconut milk (from a can)
- 1 tablespoon coconut oil
- 1 teaspoon vanilla extract
- Pinch of salt
- Optional coatings: Cocoa powder, finely chopped nuts (such as almonds or hazelnuts), shredded coconut, powdered sugar, or melted dairy-free chocolate for dipping

Instructions:

1. Prepare the chocolate:
    - Place the finely chopped dark chocolate in a heatproof bowl.
2. Heat the coconut milk:
    - In a small saucepan, heat the coconut milk and coconut oil over medium heat until it starts to simmer. Do not let it boil.
3. Pour over the chocolate:
    - Pour the hot coconut milk mixture over the chopped chocolate. Let it sit undisturbed for 2-3 minutes to soften the chocolate.
4. Stir until smooth:
    - Gently stir the mixture with a spatula or whisk until the chocolate is completely melted and smooth. If needed, you can place the bowl over a saucepan of simmering water (double boiler method) to help melt the chocolate completely.
5. Add vanilla and salt:
    - Stir in the vanilla extract and a pinch of salt. Mix until well combined.
6. Chill the mixture:
    - Cover the bowl with plastic wrap, pressing it directly onto the surface of the chocolate mixture to prevent a skin from forming. Refrigerate the mixture for at least 2 hours, or until firm enough to scoop.
7. Shape the truffles:
    - Once chilled and firm, use a small spoon or a melon baller to scoop out portions of the chocolate mixture. Roll each portion into smooth balls between your palms. If the mixture gets too soft, you can refrigerate it again for a short while.
8. Coat the truffles:
    - Roll each truffle in your desired coatings such as cocoa powder, finely chopped nuts, shredded coconut, or powdered sugar. Alternatively, you can dip them in melted dairy-free chocolate for a thicker coating.
9. Chill again (optional):
    - Place the coated truffles on a baking sheet lined with parchment paper and refrigerate for about 15-30 minutes to set.
10. Serve and store:

- Arrange the vegan chocolate truffles on a serving platter or in mini cupcake liners. Store any leftover truffles in an airtight container in the refrigerator for up to 2 weeks.

Tips:

- Chocolate quality: Use high-quality dairy-free dark chocolate for the best flavor. Check the label to ensure it's vegan-friendly.
- Texture: If the chocolate mixture is too firm after chilling, let it sit at room temperature for a few minutes to soften slightly before shaping.
- Variations: Feel free to customize your truffles by adding flavors like espresso powder, almond extract, or citrus zest to the chocolate mixture before chilling.

These vegan chocolate truffles are perfect for indulging in a rich and creamy chocolatey treat without dairy. Enjoy making and sharing these delicious truffles with friends and family!

Strawberry Basil Gelato

Ingredients:

- 1 pound fresh strawberries, hulled and sliced
- 1 cup granulated sugar
- 1/4 cup fresh basil leaves, chopped
- 2 cups whole milk
- 1 cup heavy cream
- Pinch of salt
- 1 teaspoon vanilla extract

Instructions:

1. Prepare the strawberries:
   - In a medium saucepan, combine the sliced strawberries, granulated sugar, and chopped basil leaves. Heat over medium-low heat, stirring occasionally, until the strawberries release their juices and become soft and syrupy, about 10-15 minutes.
2. Blend the strawberry mixture:
   - Remove the strawberry mixture from heat and let it cool slightly. Transfer the mixture to a blender or food processor and blend until smooth.
3. Strain (optional):
   - For a smoother gelato, strain the blended strawberry mixture through a fine-mesh sieve into a bowl to remove the seeds and any solids. Use a spatula to press the mixture through the sieve.
4. Prepare the base:
   - In a clean saucepan, combine the whole milk, heavy cream, and pinch of salt. Heat over medium heat until it just begins to simmer, stirring occasionally. Do not boil.
5. Combine with the strawberry mixture:
   - Remove the milk mixture from heat and stir in the blended strawberry mixture and vanilla extract until well combined.
6. Chill the mixture:
   - Cover the bowl with plastic wrap, pressing it directly onto the surface of the gelato base to prevent a skin from forming. Refrigerate the mixture for at least 4 hours, or preferably overnight, until thoroughly chilled.
7. Churn the gelato:
   - Pour the chilled gelato mixture into an ice cream maker and churn according to the manufacturer's instructions until it reaches a soft-serve consistency.
8. Freeze the gelato:
   - Transfer the churned gelato into a freezer-safe container. Smooth the top with a spatula. Cover with parchment paper or plastic wrap directly on the surface of the

gelato to prevent ice crystals from forming. Freeze for at least 4 hours or until firm.
9. Serve:
    - Scoop the Strawberry Basil Gelato into bowls or cones. Garnish with fresh basil leaves or sliced strawberries if desired. Enjoy this refreshing and flavorful frozen treat!

Tips:

- Strawberries: Use ripe, sweet strawberries for the best flavor. If fresh strawberries are not in season, you can use frozen strawberries that have been thawed.
- Basil: Adjust the amount of basil to taste. You can increase or decrease the amount depending on how strong you want the basil flavor to be.
- Storage: Store any leftover gelato in an airtight container in the freezer for up to 1-2 weeks. Allow it to soften slightly at room temperature for a few minutes before scooping and serving.

This Strawberry Basil Gelato is a perfect balance of fruity sweetness with a hint of herbal freshness from the basil, making it a unique and delightful dessert option for warm days or any occasion. Enjoy the creamy texture and vibrant flavors of this homemade gelato!

Apple Cinnamon Rice Pudding

Ingredients:

- 1 cup Arborio rice (or any short-grain rice)
- 4 cups milk (dairy or non-dairy such as almond milk or coconut milk)
- 1/4 cup granulated sugar (adjust to taste)
- 1 teaspoon vanilla extract
- 2 medium apples, peeled, cored, and diced
- 1 teaspoon ground cinnamon
- Pinch of salt
- Optional toppings: Chopped nuts (such as almonds or walnuts), raisins, additional cinnamon for dusting

Instructions:

1. Cook the rice:
   - In a medium saucepan, combine the rice and milk. Bring to a boil over medium-high heat, then reduce the heat to low. Simmer gently, stirring occasionally, until the rice is tender and the mixture has thickened, about 20-25 minutes.
2. Add sugar and vanilla:
   - Stir in the granulated sugar and vanilla extract into the rice pudding mixture. Continue to cook for another 5-10 minutes, stirring occasionally, until the pudding reaches your desired consistency.
3. Cook the apples:
   - While the rice pudding is cooking, heat a separate skillet over medium heat. Add the diced apples, ground cinnamon, and a pinch of salt. Cook, stirring occasionally, until the apples are tender and caramelized, about 5-7 minutes.
4. Combine the apple mixture:
   - Once the rice pudding is cooked to your liking, remove it from the heat. Fold in the cooked apple mixture until evenly distributed.
5. Serve:
   - Spoon the apple cinnamon rice pudding into serving bowls or dishes. Serve warm, sprinkled with additional cinnamon if desired, and top with chopped nuts or raisins for added texture.
6. Optional: Chill and serve cold:
   - If you prefer, you can refrigerate the rice pudding until chilled before serving. It can be enjoyed cold as well.

Tips:

- Rice: Arborio rice works well for its creamy texture, but you can use other short-grain rice varieties if preferred.

- Apples: Use sweet and firm apples such as Honeycrisp or Fuji for best results. Adjust the sweetness according to the natural sweetness of the apples and your preference.
- Variations: Add a splash of apple cider or apple juice to enhance the apple flavor. You can also stir in a tablespoon of butter or coconut oil for added richness.

This apple cinnamon rice pudding is a comforting dessert that's perfect for cooler days or as a sweet ending to any meal. Enjoy the warm flavors of cinnamon-spiced apples combined with creamy rice pudding!

Blueberry Cheesecake Bites

Ingredients:

- 1 cup graham cracker crumbs
- 3 tablespoons unsalted butter, melted
- 8 ounces cream cheese, softened
- 1/4 cup powdered sugar
- 1/2 teaspoon vanilla extract
- 1/2 cup fresh blueberries
- Fresh mint leaves, for garnish (optional)

Instructions:

1. Prepare the crust:
   - In a medium bowl, combine the graham cracker crumbs and melted butter. Stir until the crumbs are evenly coated with butter.
2. Form the crust base:
   - Line a mini muffin tin with mini cupcake liners. Place a small spoonful of the graham cracker mixture into each liner. Press down firmly with the back of a spoon to form a compact crust base. Chill in the refrigerator while preparing the filling.
3. Make the cheesecake filling:
   - In a mixing bowl, beat the softened cream cheese until smooth and creamy using a hand mixer or stand mixer.
   - Add the powdered sugar and vanilla extract to the cream cheese. Beat again until well combined and smooth.
4. Assemble the blueberry cheesecake bites:
   - Spoon or pipe the cheesecake filling evenly into each prepared graham cracker crust in the mini muffin tin.
   - Gently press 2-3 fresh blueberries into the top of each cheesecake bite, slightly submerging them into the filling.
5. Chill the bites:
   - Refrigerate the blueberry cheesecake bites for at least 2 hours, or until the cheesecake filling is firm.
6. Serve:
   - Once chilled and set, carefully remove the cheesecake bites from the mini muffin tin. Garnish with fresh mint leaves if desired.
7. Enjoy:
   - Serve these delicious blueberry cheesecake bites chilled as a delightful mini-dessert for any occasion!

Tips:

- Graham cracker crumbs: You can buy pre-crushed graham cracker crumbs or crush them yourself using a food processor or by placing them in a plastic bag and crushing with a rolling pin.
- Variations: Instead of blueberries, you can use other berries such as raspberries or strawberries. You can also add a drizzle of melted chocolate or a dollop of fruit preserves on top for extra flavor.
- Storage: Store the blueberry cheesecake bites in an airtight container in the refrigerator. They are best enjoyed within a few days of making.

These blueberry cheesecake bites are perfect for parties, gatherings, or as a sweet treat for yourself. They offer a creamy cheesecake texture with a burst of fresh blueberry flavor in every bite!

Chocolate Mint Avocado Cookies

Ingredients:

- 1 ripe avocado, mashed (about 1/2 cup)
- 1/2 cup coconut sugar (or granulated sugar)
- 1/4 cup cocoa powder
- 1/2 teaspoon vanilla extract
- 1/4 teaspoon peppermint extract
- 1/4 teaspoon salt
- 1/2 teaspoon baking soda
- 1 cup almond flour
- 1/2 cup dairy-free chocolate chips (optional)

Instructions:

1. Preheat the oven:
   - Preheat your oven to 350°F (175°C). Line a baking sheet with parchment paper or silicone baking mat.
2. Mix wet ingredients:
   - In a mixing bowl, combine the mashed avocado, coconut sugar, vanilla extract, and peppermint extract. Mix until well combined and smooth.
3. Add dry ingredients:
   - Add the cocoa powder, salt, baking soda, and almond flour to the avocado mixture. Stir until everything is well combined and forms a thick dough.
4. Fold in chocolate chips (optional):
   - If using chocolate chips, fold them into the cookie dough until evenly distributed.
5. Form cookies:
   - Scoop about 1 tablespoon of dough and roll it into a ball. Place it on the prepared baking sheet and flatten slightly with the palm of your hand. Repeat with the remaining dough, spacing the cookies about 2 inches apart.
6. Bake:
   - Bake in the preheated oven for 10-12 minutes, or until the edges are set. The cookies will still be soft in the center but will firm up as they cool.
7. Cool and enjoy:
   - Remove from the oven and let the cookies cool on the baking sheet for 5 minutes before transferring them to a wire rack to cool completely.
8. Store:
   - Store the chocolate mint avocado cookies in an airtight container at room temperature for up to 3-4 days. For longer storage, keep them in the refrigerator.

Tips:

- Avocado: Make sure your avocado is ripe and mashed well to ensure a smooth texture in the cookies.
- Sweetness: Adjust the amount of coconut sugar according to your preference. You can also use other sweeteners like maple syrup or honey if desired.
- Texture: The almond flour gives these cookies a soft and slightly crumbly texture. If you prefer a firmer cookie, you can mix in some oat flour or additional almond flour.
- Variations: Instead of chocolate chips, you can add chopped nuts or dried fruit for added texture and flavor.

These chocolate mint avocado cookies are a nutritious and delicious treat, perfect for satisfying your sweet tooth with a hint of minty freshness!

Coconut Flour Donuts

Ingredients:

For the donuts:

- 1/2 cup coconut flour
- 1/4 cup granulated sugar (or sweetener of choice)
- 1/2 teaspoon baking powder
- 1/4 teaspoon baking soda
- Pinch of salt
- 4 large eggs
- 1/4 cup coconut oil, melted
- 1/2 cup coconut milk (or any milk of choice)
- 1 teaspoon vanilla extract

For the glaze (optional):

- 1/2 cup powdered sugar (or powdered sweetener)
- 2-3 tablespoons coconut milk (or any milk of choice)
- 1/2 teaspoon vanilla extract
- Shredded coconut, for topping (optional)

Instructions:

1. Preheat the oven:
   - Preheat your oven to 350°F (175°C). Grease a donut pan with coconut oil or non-stick cooking spray.
2. Mix dry ingredients:
   - In a mixing bowl, whisk together the coconut flour, granulated sugar, baking powder, baking soda, and salt until well combined.
3. Combine wet ingredients:
   - In a separate bowl, whisk together the eggs, melted coconut oil, coconut milk, and vanilla extract until smooth.
4. Make the batter:
   - Pour the wet ingredients into the bowl with the dry ingredients. Stir until just combined and no lumps remain. Let the batter sit for a few minutes to allow the coconut flour to absorb the liquid and thicken.
5. Fill the donut pan:
   - Spoon the batter into a piping bag or a zip-top bag with a corner snipped off. Pipe the batter evenly into the prepared donut pan, filling each mold about 3/4 full.
6. Bake the donuts:
   - Bake in the preheated oven for 15-18 minutes, or until the donuts are set and lightly golden brown on top. Insert a toothpick into the center of a donut to check for doneness; it should come out clean.

7. Cool the donuts:
   - Remove the donut pan from the oven and let the donuts cool in the pan for 5 minutes. Then, transfer them to a wire rack to cool completely.
8. Glaze the donuts (optional):
   - In a shallow bowl, whisk together the powdered sugar, coconut milk, and vanilla extract until smooth. Dip each cooled donut into the glaze, allowing any excess to drip off. Place the glazed donuts back on the wire rack.
9. Top with shredded coconut (optional):
   - If desired, sprinkle shredded coconut over the glazed donuts while the glaze is still wet.
10. Serve and enjoy:
    - Let the glaze set for a few minutes before serving. Enjoy these coconut flour donuts as a delicious treat!

Tips:

- Donut pan: If you don't have a donut pan, you can make these as muffins instead. Adjust the baking time as needed.
- Storage: Store leftover coconut flour donuts in an airtight container at room temperature for up to 3 days. You can also freeze them (unglazed) for longer storage.
- Flavor variations: Add a teaspoon of cinnamon or nutmeg to the batter for spiced donuts. You can also fold in chocolate chips or dried fruit for added texture and flavor.

These coconut flour donuts are light, fluffy, and perfect for anyone looking for a gluten-free and healthier alternative to traditional donuts. Enjoy making and indulging in these delicious treats!